What Every Environmentalist Needs
to Know about Capitalism

What Every Environmentalist Needs to Know about Capitalism

A Citizen's Guide to Capitalism and the Environment

Fred Magdoff *and* John Bellamy Foster

MONTHLY REVIEW PRESS

New York

Library of Congress Cataloging-in-Publication Data

Magdoff, Fred, 1942–

  What every environmentalist needs to know about capitalism : a citizen's guide to capitalism and the environment / Fred Magdoff and John Bellamy Foster.

    p. cm.

  Includes bibliographical references and index.

  ISBN 978-1-58367-241-9 (pbk. : alk. paper) — ISBN 978-1-58367-242-6 (cloth : alk. paper) 1. Environmental economics. 2. Capitalism. 3. Environmentalism—Economic aspects. 4. Environmentalism—Political aspects. 5. Environmental policy. I. Foster, John Bellamy. II. Title.

  HC79.E5M329 2011

  330.12'2—dc23

                          2011021515

Monthly Review Press

146 West 29th Street, Suite 6W

New York, New York 10001

www.monthlyreview.org

www.MRzine.org

5 4 3 2

Contents

Preface

> Wealth, if limits are not set for it, is great poverty.
>
> —EPICURUS[1]

Ecological economist Herman Daly is well known for emphasizing what he has called the "Impossibility Theorem" of unlimited economic growth in a limited environment. Put concretely, an extension of a U.S.-style high consumption economy to the entire world of 7 billion people—much less the 9 billion-plus world population projected for the middle of the present century—is a flat impossibility.[2] In this book we are concerned with extending Daly's Impossibility Theorem by introducing what we regard to be its most important corollary: the continuation for any length of time of capitalism, as a grow-or-die system dedicated to unlimited capital accumulation, is itself a flat impossibility.

We are constantly being told by the vested interests—and even by self-designated environmentalists and environmental organizations—that capitalism offers the solution to the environmental problem: as if the further growth of capital markets, green consumption, and new technology provide us with miraculous ways out of our global ecological dilemma. Such views are rooted in an absolute denial of reality, or what John Kenneth Galbraith has called a system of "innocent fraud."[3] In this make-believe, *Through the Looking Glass* world, the wondrous work-ings of markets, perhaps tweaked here or there by regulations and incentives, make miracles possible. In the process, the laws of physics, chemistry, biology, and ecology—as well as the limits of the earth—are simply conjured away. Fundamental changes in our mode of existence and our lifestyle are not required: another world is not necessary.

All of this raises questions about what constitutes environ-mentalism. Today, more people than ever are convinced that the degradation of the earth's life support systems is leading us toward catastrophe. Whether they are environmental activists or not, growing numbers of people are concerned about the environ-ment and are taking small steps, and willing to do much more, in order to protect the planet. For all those concerned with the fate of the earth, the time has come to face facts: not simply the dire reality of climate change and other forms of environmental destruction, but also that there is a pressing need to change the basic relationships between humanity and the earth. Put simply, it is essential to break with a system based on a single motive—the perpetual accumulation of capital, and hence economic growth without end. Such a break is a necessary, if not sufficient, condi-tion for the creation of a new ecological civilization.

This book grew out of an article with the same title, originally published in the March 2010 issue of *Monthly Review*.[4] Interest in our article was so great that we were encouraged to expand it into a short book. This brief work thus is a product of its origins. We have not tried to present a systematic discussion of the entire planetary ecological crisis, though many aspects of that are touched on here.[5] Rather our goal is to provide a useful introduc-tion to the issue laid out in our title: *What Every Environmentalist Needs to Know about Capitalism*. What every environmentalist needs to know, of course, is that capitalism is not the solution but the problem, and that if humanity is going to survive this crisis, it will do so because it has exercised its capacity for human freedom, through social struggle, in order to create a whole new world—in coevolution with the planet.

Our personal and intellectual debts in relation to this work are too vast to acknowledge in full. However, we would like to thank especially Hannah Holleman and Jan Schultz, who aided and assisted us in the preparation of the present manuscript at various stages of completion.

We would also like to acknowledge the political and intellectual support of those at *Monthly Review*, Monthly Review Press, and *MRzine*, without which this work would have been inconceivable, including: Scott Borchert, Brett Clark, Susie Day, Yoshie Furushashi, John Mage, Martin Paddio, John Simon, Victor Wallis, and Michael Yates.

Some of our close friends, colleagues, and students have contributed to our understanding of ecological issues in ways that have impacted this book: including Matthew Clement, Cade Jameson, R. Jamil Jonna, Brian Tokar, Ryan Wishart, and Richard York.

During the last two years, while working on the ideas in this book, we have traveled to Bolivia, Brazil, China, Venezuela, and Vietnam to discuss ecological issues. We are thus constantly reminded that the ecological movement is a planetary one. We would like to thank the many individuals from many different cultures that we have encountered in these journeys.

Finally, we would like to offer our heartfelt thanks to Amy Demarest and Carrie Ann Naumoff, with whom we share our lives on this earth and our struggles for a sustainable future.

JUNE 5, 2011
FLETCHER, VERMONT
EUGENE, OREGON

1. The Planetary Ecological Crisis

> Let us not, however, flatter ourselves overmuch on account of
> our human victories over nature. For each such victory nature
> takes its revenge on us. Each victory, it is true, in the first place
> brings about the results we expected, but in the second and
> third places it has quite different, unforeseen effects which only
> too often cancel the first.
>
> —FREDERICK ENGELS[1]

Environmental degradation is not new to today's world but has
occurred throughout recorded history with profound negative consequences for a number of ancient civilizations—most notably
Mesopotamia and the Maya, which experienced major collapses due
to what are believed to be ecological causes. Problems with deforestation, soil erosion, and salinization of irrigated soils were present
throughout antiquity. Commenting on the ecological destruction in
ancient Greece Plato (c. 427–347 BCE) wrote in *Critias*:

> What proof then can we offer that it [the land in the vicinity of
> Athens] is . . . now a mere remnant of what it once was? . . . You
> are left (as with little islands) with something rather like the skele-

ton of a body wasted by disease; the rich, soft soil has all run away leaving the land nothing but skin and bone. . . . For some mountains which today will only support bees produced not so long ago trees which when cut provided roof beams for huge buildings whose roofs are still standing. And there were a lot of tall cultivated trees which bore unlimited quantities of fodder for beasts. The soil benefitted from an annual rainfall which did not run to waste off the bare earth as it does today, but was absorbed in large quantities and stored in retentive layers of clay, so that what was drunk down by the higher regions flowed downwards into the valleys and appeared everywhere in a multitude of rivers and springs. And the shrines which still survive at these former springs are proof of the truth of our present account of the country.[2]

What makes the modern era stand out in this respect, however, is that there are many more of us inhabiting more of the earth; we have technologies that can do much greater damage and do it more quickly; *and* we have an economic system that knows no bounds. The damage being done today is so widespread that it not only degrades local and regional ecologies, as in earlier civilizations, but also affects the planetary environment, threatening the existence of a majority of species on the planet, including our own. There are therefore sound, scientific reasons to be concerned about the current rapid degradation of the earth's environment.

What we call *the* environmental problem today is not reducible to a single issue no matter how large, but rather consists of a complex of problems. One of the latest, most important developments in Earth system science, developed by leading scientists, is the concept of "planetary boundaries," in which nine critical boundaries/thresholds of the earth system have been designated (or are being considered) in relation to: (1) climate change; (2) ocean acidification; (3) stratospheric ozone depletion; (4) the biogeochemical flow boundary (the nitrogen and phosphorus cycles); (5) global freshwater use; (6) change in land use; (7) biodiversity loss; (8) atmospheric aerosol loading; and (9) chemical pollution. Staying within each of these boundaries is considered essential to maintaining the relatively benign climate and environmental conditions that have existed during the last 12,000 years (the Holocene epoch). The sustainable boundaries in three of these systems—climate change, biodiversity, and human interference with the nitrogen cycle (part of the biogeochemical flow boundary)—have already been crossed, representing extreme rifts in the Earth system, while others—ocean acidification, global freshwater use, changes in land use, and the phosphorus cycle—represent emerging rifts. (Proposed boundaries for atmospheric aerosol loading and chemical pollution have yet to be designated.)[3]

Although each of these rifts in planetary boundaries constitutes a major threat to life on the planet as we know it, it is climate change that is the biggest, most immediate threat, occupying a particularly central place, since it overlaps with all the others. Human-induced increases in greenhouse gases (carbon dioxide, methane, nitrous oxide, etc.) are destabilizing the world's climate. If humanity does not soon change course, this will probably have horrendous effects for most species on the planet, including our own. Each decade is warmer than the one before, with 2010 tying with 2005 as the warmest year in the 131 years of global instrumental temperature records, and with nine of the warmest years on record in the last decade.[4]

Indications of accelerating problems directly tied to climate change are already beginning to manifest themselves. These include:

- *Melting of the Arctic Ocean ice during the summer, which reduces the reflection of sunlight, thereby enhancing global warming.* Satellites show that end-of-summer Arctic sea ice was 40 percent less in 2007 than in the late 1970s when accurate measurements began.[5] The three years with the least Arctic Sea ice cover at the end of summer were 2007, 2008, and 2010.[6]

- *A rise in sea level that has averaged 1.7 millimeters (mm) per year since 1875, but which since 1993 has averaged 3 mm per year, or over an inch per decade, with the prospect that the rate will increase further.* The eventual disintegration of the Greenland and Antarctic ice sheets, set in motion by global warming, may result in a huge rise in ocean levels. Even a sea level rise of one to two meters would be disastrous for hundreds of millions of people in low-lying countries such as Bangladesh, Vietnam, and various island states. At present, the Arctic Monitoring and Assessment Program, the scientific arm of the eight-nation Arctic Council, is projecting rises in sea level by as much as just over a meter and a half this century based on current trends.[7] A sea level rise at a rate of a few meters per century is not unusual in the paleoclimatic record. At present, more than 400 million people live within five meters of sea level, and more than one billion within 25 meters.[8]

- *The rapid decrease of the world's mountain glaciers, many of which—if business-as-usual greenhouse gas emissions continue—could largely be gone during this century.* Some 90 percent of mountain glaciers worldwide are already visibly retreating as the planet warms. The Himalayan glaciers provide dry season water to hundreds of millions of people in Asia; their shrinking will lead to floods and acute water scarcity. Already the melting of the Andean glaciers is contributing to floods in that region. In April 2010 some fifty people were injured in Peru as part of a glacier fell into a glacial lake, causing the Hualcan River coming from the lake to overflow its banks.[9] But the most immediate, current, and long-term problem, associated with disappearing glaciers—visible today in Bolivia and Peru—is that of water shortages, because the glaciers function as water storage reservoirs.[10]

- *Warming of the oceans, where some 90 percent of the heat added to the planet has accumulated.* This has been implicated in a dramatic decrease in the phytoplankton (microscopic plant-like organisms) that are at the bottom of the ocean food chain—with much of the decline occurring in the last fifty years.[11] Although other causes besides global warming may be involved (see discussion of ocean acidification below), such a remarkable decline of productivity at the base of the ocean's food chain will undoubtedly have a profound negative effect on the future overall productivity of the seas.

- *Devastating droughts, expanding possibly to 70 percent of the land area within several decades under business as usual.* Effects are already evident in northern India and northeast Africa; while Australia experienced a ten-year drought in the opening decade of this century (with the rains only just returning).[12] But even when rains come, they frequently are so intense that flooding and loss of life occurs, as with the 2010 floods in Pakistan and the 2011 floods in Australia. As reported in the *Independent* (UK) with respect to Pakistan: "The twin hazards of perilously low levels of water for most of the year followed by summer weeks of calamitous flooding illustrate the scale of the problem for countries such as Pakistan. It is often the same countries that suffer limited supplies of clean water that also endure flood devastation."[13]

- *Warmer winter and summer temperatures that have already upset regional ecosystems.* One example concerns the white bark pine tree that normally grows to a very old age—with some over a thousand years old—on the upper elevations of the western mountains in the United States. These stands have provided habitat and food for many species of birds and mammals, including bears. The pine bark beetle, now able to reproduce at the higher elevations because of warmer temperatures, is infesting these zones and turning huge areas of white bark pine trees into "ghost forests." The death of the forests in turn means no food for the animals, forcing them to move to lower elevations. In addition, snow melts more quickly in the dead forests, causing faster melt and runoff in the spring and low and warm rivers in the summer, with adverse effects on fish.[14]

- *Negative effects on crop yields as average global temperature rises.* Higher levels of CO_2 in the atmosphere may increase the production of some types of crops, but they may then be harmed in future years by a destabilized climate that brings either dry or very wet conditions. Losses in rice yields have already been measured in parts of Southeast Asia, attributed to higher night temperatures which cause the plant to undergo enhanced nighttime respiration. This means that plants at night lose more of what they produced by photosynthesis during the day.[15] A study in Africa found that for each day the temperature was above 30° C (86° F) corn yields decreased by one percent if plentiful water was available and by 1.7 percent under drought conditions.[16] A study of climate and agricultural production since 1980 indicates that detectable decreases in global corn and wheat production are already occurring due to changes in climate.[17]

- *Extinction of species due to rapid shifts in climate zones or "isotherms"—regions in which a given average temperature prevails and to which specific species are adapted.* Studies of more than a thousand species of plants, animals, and insects have found that whereas the average migration to the north and south (toward the poles) was four miles per decade in the second half of the twentieth century, isotherms have been "outrunning" species, moving poleward at a rate of about 35 miles per decade over the last thirty years. At the same time species that live at the poles (such as polar bears) and in alpine regions have nowhere to move and are simply being run off the earth.[18]

All of this points to the fact that climate change does not occur in a gradual way, with equal change each year, but rather takes the form of tipping points fed by amplifying feedbacks that can hasten change and its consequences. Seen in this way, the melting of Arctic ice is an "amplifying feedback." The rapid melting of white ice and its replacement with blue seawater is decreasing the earth's reflectivity (the albedo effect) resulting in the absorption of additional radiation and the acceleration of global warming. Such amplifying feedbacks shorten the time separating us from major tipping points, beyond which there is no stopping a process. Such a major tipping point, as we have mentioned, is the disintegration of ice sheets in Greenland and West Antarctica, which would lead to a dramatic rise in world sea levels. Loss of the entire West Antarctic ice sheet would raise sea level by 20 to 25 feet and open the way to the ocean for the much larger East Antarctic ice sheet.[19]

Other Planetary Rifts

Climate change, as noted, is only one of a number of planetary rifts brought on by the crossing of planetary boundaries.

Like climate change, ocean acidification is a product of increased emissions of carbon dioxide. The boundary for ocean acidification, recently proposed by scientists, is determined on the basis of the global mean saturation state of aragonite (a form of calcium carbonate) in surface seawater. A decline in the number indicates an increase in the acidity of the ocean. The preindustrial value was 3.44 (surface ocean aragonite saturation state); the proposed boundary—after which there would be a massive die-down of shell-forming organisms—is 2.75; and the current state is 2.90. Ocean acidification is often referred to as the "evil twin" of climate change, since it derives from increases in carbon dioxide emissions and has equally devastating implications for the planetary system.[20]

One area that appears to have been brought under control in the 1990s, but raised serious concerns because of the rapid increase in ultraviolet radiation from the sun that was occurring up to that time, is stratospheric ozone depletion. The preindustrial value of ozone concentration was 290 (in Dobson Units—the measurement of atmospheric ozone columnar density); the proposed planetary boundary is a concentration of 276, after which life on the planet would experience devastating losses; and the current status is 283. The decline in stratospheric ozone concentrations has now been halted between 60°S and 60°N. Nevertheless, it will take decades for the Antarctic ozone hole to disappear, and Arctic ozone loss will also likely persist for decades. Life on the planet had a close call.[21]

The preindustrial annual rate of species loss, considered the "natural" or "background" rate, was 0.1–1 per million. The planetary boundary recently proposed by scientists is 10 per million, whereas the current rate is greater than 100 per million (100 to 1,000 times the preindustrial background rate).[22] Species are disappearing at accelerating rates not only because of global warming but also—more importantly at present—through direct human impact on species' habitats. We are living in an era that scientists have characterized as the "sixth extinction," which threatens to rival the great mass extinctions of the geological past, the most recent of which was the dying out of the dinosaurs 65 million years ago. The sixth extinction, emerging in our time, is distinct from these earlier mass extinctions in that it is brought on chiefly by a living species: our own.

A 2009 survey by the International Union for Conservation of Nature estimated that over 17,000 animals and plants are at risk of extinction. "More than one in five of all known mammals, over a quarter of reptiles, and 70 percent of plants are under threat, according to the survey, which featured over 2,800 new species compared with 2008. 'These results are just the tip of the iceberg,' said Craig Hilton-Taylor, who manages the list. He said many more species that have yet to be assessed could also be under serious threat."[23] As species disappear, ecosystems that depend on a multitude of species to function begin to degrade. One of the many consequences of degraded ecosystems with fewer species appears to be greater transmission of infectious diseases.[24]

The overloading of the environment with nitrogen and phosphorus runoff from fertilizers represents another ecological rift affecting the biogeochemical cycles of the planet. For nitrogen the proposed boundary introduced by scientists is concerned primarily with the amount of nitrogen removed from the atmosphere by chemical means (the Haber-Bosch process), as well as nitrogen fixation through the cultivation of legumes, in millions of tons per year. Before the rise of industrial capitalism (more specifically before the rise of the Haber-Bosch process early in the twentieth century) the amount of nitrogen removed from the atmosphere was relatively low. The proposed boundary limit to avoid global ecological degradation from excess nitrogen is 35 million tons—including both agricultural legume-fixed nitrogen and the industrial production of "fixed" nitrogen (mainly for nitrogen fertilizers)—while its current status is 121 million tons. Although the limit suggested is not sufficient to produce all the needed grain crops, it is clear that annual nitrogen fixation can, and should, be reduced significantly from its current level with better systems in place to cycle nutrients in human and animal waste back to farmland. In spite of the fact that phosphorus runoff is currently less of a threat than nitrogen, it is rapidly growing in significance. The preindustrial amount of phosphorus flowing into the oceans per year was 1 million tons. The proposed boundary is 11 million tons, while the current status is 8.5 to 9.5 million tons and rising rapidly.[25]

There are literally hundreds of locations around the world where these chemicals, flowing into the oceans, are resulting in an explosion of phytoplankton. As the massive quantities of phytoplankton die, decomposing organisms lower in the oceans create very low oxygen zones— technically referred to as hypoxic or low oxygen zones, but sometimes called "dead zones"—in which many species of fish cannot exist. One of the largest of these is the dead zone where the Mississippi River enters the Gulf of Mexico. The largest such area occurs in Europe's Baltic Sea.

The global freshwater boundary is also being transgressed. Thresholds of both blue water (liquid) flows and green water (vapor) flows are being disrupted, threatening the entire hydrological cycle. At present an estimated 25 percent of the world's river basins run dry before reaching the oceans as a result of human use of freshwater resources. The preindustrial use of freshwater was 415 km³ (cubic kilometers) per year. The proposed boundary for freshwater consumptive use recently designated by scientists (beyond which there is a significant risk of collapse of terrestrial and aquatic ecosystems on regional and continental scales) is 4,000 km³. The current status is 2,600 km³.[26]

With respect to direct human needs, the global freshwater crisis is already upon us. As Maude Barlow writes in *Blue Covenant*: "The world is facing a water crisis due to pollution, climate change and a surging population growth of such magnitude that close to two billion people now live in water-stressed regions of the planet. Further, unless we change our ways, by the year 2025, two-thirds of the world's population will face water scarcity."[27] In some areas, such as northern China, northern India, and the part of the U.S. Great Plains that sits over the Oglala aquifer, water is being pumped out faster than it can be replenished, with deeper extraction only delaying the end of these sources. In the Punjab region, which grows about half of India's grain reserves, water is being pumped out of the ground 45 percent faster than rains can replenish it[28]—a recipe for disaster.

Changes in the land use associated with human production represent a further rift in planetary boundaries. The conversion of forests and other ecosystems to agricultural land is reaching

what scientists believe to be a critical threshold, threatening biodiversity and undermining the regulatory processes of the Earth
system. For example, conversion of the Amazon rain forest into
agricultural land could reach a level where it would tip the rain
forest system into that of a semi-arid savannah. In South
America, rain forests are commonly first converted to extensive
pastures and later used for export crops such as soybeans. In
Southeast Asia land is being converted into oil palm plantations—with the oil exported as a feedstock for making biodiesel
fuel. This destruction of tropical forests, in addition to displacing the forests' indigenous people, is causing an estimated 25
percent of all human-induced release of CO_2.[29] Soil degradation
by erosion, overgrazing, and low levels of organic matter application threatens the productivity of large areas of the world's agricultural lands.

There were relatively low amounts of preindustrial anthropogenic changes in land use. The proposed boundary—a threshold the transgression of which would lead to major ecosystem dis-
ruptions globally—is 15 percent of ice-free land converted to agriculture uses. The current status of land converted for agriculture
worldwide is 12 percent.[30]

Aerosol atmospheric loading with soot, sulfates, and other
particles is viewed as a global process posing a potential planetary
boundary, but due to its complexity (and problems of measurement) a safe boundary has not been designated. Aerosols both
influence the climate system and have an adverse effect on human
health. The global concentration of most aerosols has doubled
since preindustrial times. Aerosols affect the Earth's radiation
balance by scattering incoming radiation back into space or indi-
rectly affecting cloud reflectivity and balance. Aerosols have thus
played a role in tempering climate change. They also influence
the hydrological cycle and may have a substantial effect on mon-
soons. The negative effects of aerosols on human health are substantial, resulting annually in some 800,000 premature deaths.[31]

Scientists working on planetary boundaries have not yet determined a boundary for chemical pollution due to the numerous,
complex issues involved, and the vast quantity of synthetic chemicals in use, which number in the tens of thousands (without count-
ing all the possible combinations in which these chemicals interact
in the environment, which are astronomical in number).
Nevertheless, it is clear that the spread of chemical pollution in the
form of radioactive compounds, heavy metals, and a wide range of
organic compounds introduced by industry represents a threat to
biodiversity, to human life, and interacts in complex ways with
other global environmental stresses such as climate change.[32] Some
of these chemical pollutants, such as the metal mercury, go up
smokestacks to later fall and contaminate soil and water, while others are leached into surface waters from waste storage facilities.

Many ocean and freshwater fish are contaminated with mercury, as well as numerous industrial organic chemicals. The
oceans contain large "islands" of trash of various kinds, though
predominantly plastics, the product of the petrochemical industry. "Light bulbs, bottle caps, toothbrushes, Popsicle sticks and
tiny pieces of plastic, each the size of a grain of rice, inhabit the
Pacific garbage patch, an area of widely dispersed trash that dou-
bles in size every decade and is now believed to be roughly twice
the size of Texas."[33] Sunlight and warm temperatures partially
degrade the massive amount of plastic in the oceans into ever-
smaller particles. There is so much of this material in the seas that
"a handful of sand or cup of sea water from nearly anywhere in
the world will probably be peppered with microplastics—pieces
that are tinier than a small pea and often invisible."[34] These small
pieces of plastic can harm small animals at the bottom of the food
web as the plastic degrades within the organism and may do even
more damage because it absorbs and concentrates toxic chemicals in the water.

In the United States, drinking water used by millions of people is polluted with pesticides such as atrazine, as well as nitrates

and other contaminants of industrial agriculture. We are all contaminated by a variety of industrial and agricultural chemicals,
and there is great concern about the health consequences.
Agricultural pesticides are of special concern for people working
with them or living in areas in which they are widely used.
However, many foods we eat are also contaminated with pesticides. For example, more than half of the frozen blueberries and
nearly half of the strawberries tested by the U.S. Department of
Agriculture had detectable levels of a fungicide (boscalid); over
half of the strawberries contained detectable levels of the fungicide captan; 50 percent of the grape juice tested contained the
insecticide carbaryl; 75 percent of potatoes tested positive for the
herbicide chlorpropham; about half of the green onions, collards,
and kale tested positive for the herbicide DCPA; 40 percent of the
sweet potatoes tested positive for the fungicide dicloran; almost
70 percent of broccoli tested positive for the insecticide imidaclo-
prid; and 40 percent of summer squash tested positive for the
insecticide endosulphan. Some produce was contaminated with
multiple chemicals. For example, from 20 to 100 percent of strawberries tested positive for each of sixteen different pesticides. And
the list goes on and on.[35]

A survey of twenty physicians and nurses who were tested for
sixty-two chemicals in blood and urine—mostly organic chemicals such as flame retardants and plasticizers—found that "each
participant had at least 24 individual chemicals in their body, and
two participants had a high of 39 chemicals detected. . . . All participants had bisphenol A" (BPA), a suspected carcinogen, used
to make rigid polycarbonate plastics used in water cooler bottles,
baby bottles, linings of most metal food containers—and present
in the foods inside these containers, kitchen appliances, and the
thermal paper receipts people receive from supermarkets, automatic teller machines, gas stations, etc. Likewise each had: (1)
some form of phthalates, found in many consumer products such
as hair sprays, cosmetics, plastic products, and wood finishers;

(2) PBDEs (polybrominated diphenyl ethers), used as flame retardants in computers, furniture, mattresses, and medical equipment; and (3) PFCs (perfluorinated compounds), used in nonstick pans, protective coatings for carpets, paper coatings, etc.[36]

Although physicians and nurses are routinely exposed to larger quantities of certain chemicals than the general public, we are all exposed to these and other chemicals that don't belong in our bodies, and that most likely have negative effects on human health. Some 93 percent of people in the United States have BPA byproducts in their urine. Almost all people in the United States have detectable levels of PBDEs in their bodies. These chemicals have been shown to have negative neurological and fertility effects in animals and may lower fertility in humans as well.[37] There is significant concern that chemical contamination of fetuses during pregnancy is contributing to the rise of autism in children.[38] There also appears to be a link between organophosphate pesticides and the development of Attention-Deficit/Hyperactivity Disorder (ADHD) in children.[39]

There are more than 80,000 chemicals in commercial use in the United States, and we do not know the composition and potential harmfulness of about 20,000 of them—their composition falls under the category of "trade secrets" and is legally withheld.[40] According to an editorial in *Scientific American*, "Of the more than 80,000 chemicals in use in the U.S., only five have been either restricted or banned. Not 5 percent, *five*. The EPA has been able to force health and safety testing for only around 200."[41] At the end of March 2010, the U.S. Environmental Protection Agency finally listed BPA as a "chemical of concern," meaning that the agency will *commence* studying it.[42] The United States continues to have one of the worst records among industrialized countries concerning protection of its citizens from toxic chemicals found in products in everyday use—from cosmetics to food containers to denture cream (containing zinc that has caused toxicity in users). The use of untested and unregulated chemicals might change in the future, but not because of a change of heart by the business community regarding the poisons in their products. "The chemical industry seems less opposed to a regulatory overhaul [than in the past], in part because lax regulation may help low-cost Chinese chemical companies more than American firms."[43]

The President's Cancer Panel, in its 2010 report, summarized the situation as follows:

> A growing body of research documents myriad established and suspected environmental factors linked to genetic, immune, and endocrine dysfunction that can lead to cancer and other diseases. . . . Weak laws and regulations, inefficient enforcement, regulatory complexity, and fragmented authority allow avoidable exposures to known or suspected cancer-causing and cancer-promoting agents to continue and proliferate in the workplace and the community.[44]

It is beyond debate that the ecology of Earth—including the life support systems on which humans and all other species depend—is under sustained and severe attack by human activities. It is also clear that if we don't radically change our ways, the results will be devastating. The multifaceted, complex, and rapidly accelerating character of the planetary environmental crisis is traceable to a single systemic cause: the economic and social order in which we live. The principal cause of ecological degradation, insisted Rachel Carson, author of the classic work *Silent Spring*, which sparked the modern environmental movement, is a society that worships "the gods of speed and quantity, and of the quick and easy profit, and out of this idolatry monstrous evils have arisen."[45]

2. Business as Usual: The Road to Planetary Destruction

If the environment is polluted and the economy is sick, the virus that causes both will be found in the system of production.

—BARRY COMMONER[1]

We strongly agree with those environmentalists who have concluded that continuing "business as usual" is the path to global disaster. To many people, this means that we must limit the ecological footprint of human beings on the earth, and to do this, we need an economy—particularly in the rich countries—that ceases to grow. If world output keeps expanding and everyone in the developing countries seeks to attain the average standard of living of the wealthy capitalist states—while the latter try to enlarge their already considerable per capita wealth—not only will pollution continue to increase beyond what the Earth system can absorb, but we will also run out of limited nonrenewable resources. Both the environmental sink (or the capacity of the planet to absorb waste) and its tap (the supply of critical nonrenewable resources) will come up against absolute limits. In this connection, the authors of the well-known book *The Limits to Growth* (1972) came to the following prescient conclusions:

1. If the present growth trends in world population, industrialization, pollution, food production, and resource depletion continue unchanged, the limits to growth on this planet will be reached sometime within the next one hundred years. The most probable result will be a rather sudden and uncontrollable decline in both population and industrial capacity.

2. It is possible to alter these growth trends and to establish a condition of ecological and economic stability that is sustainable far into the future. The state of global equilibrium could be designed so that the basic material needs of each person on Earth are satisfied and each person has an equal opportunity to realize his individual human potential.

3. If the world's people decide to strive for this second outcome rather than the first, the sooner they begin working to attain it, the greater will be their chances of success.[2]

It is clear that there are biospheric limits, and that the planet cannot support the seven billion people already alive (not to mention the nine billion projected for midcentury or the ten billion projected for the end of the century) at what is known as a Western, "middle-class" standard of living. The Worldwatch Institute has estimated that a world that drew on the planet's resources per person at the level of the contemporary United States could only support 1.4 billion people.[3] Of course not everyone in the United States, where income and wealth inequality have reached stratospheric levels, lives at an equally high standard of living. Indeed, a mere 400 individuals in the United States in the year 2007 (the so-called "Forbes 400") owned nearly as much wealth as the bottom half of the country, some 150 million people.[4]

The primary problem is an ancient one and lies not with those who do not have enough for a decent standard of living, but rather with those for whom there is never enough. Epicurus said that there is no such thing as "enough to someone for whom enough is little."[5] A global social system organized on the basis of "enough is little" is bound eventually to destroy everything around it and itself as well.

Environmentalists commonly raise the issue of environmental injustice when approaching this problem, since so many of the poor are living under dangerously precarious conditions, have been especially hard hit by environmental disaster and degradation, and promise to be the main victims if current trends are allowed to continue. It is clear that approximately half of humanity—over three billion people, living in deep poverty and subsisting on less than $2.50 a day—need to have access to the requirements for a basic human existence such as decent housing, a secure food supply, clean water, and medical care. We wholeheartedly agree with all of these concerns.[6]

The Meaning of Business as Usual

It is clear that we need to change course and do so drastically and quickly. As James Gustave "Gus" Speth, one of the most prominent U.S. environmentalists and former chairman of the Council of Environmental Quality in the Carter administration, has written: "All that human societies have to do to destroy the planet's climate and biota and leave a ruined world to future generations is to keep doing exactly what is being done today, with no growth in the human population or the world economy."[7] The question is, what does not doing business as usual mean? Some environmentalists feel that it is possible to solve most of our problems by tinkering with our economic system, introducing greater energy efficiency, and substituting "green" energy sources for fossil fuels or coming up with technologies to ameliorate the problems (such as using carbon capture from power plants and injecting it deep into the earth).

Within the environmental movement, however, there are some for whom it is clear that mere economic tinkering and technical adjustments will not be enough to solve the dramatic and potentially catastrophic problems we face. Curtis White, for example, begins an article in *Orion* with this: "There is a fundamental question that environmentalists are not very good at asking, let alone answering: 'Why is this, the destruction of the natural world, happening?'"[8] It is impossible to find real and lasting solutions until we are able satisfactorily to answer this question.

It is our contention that most of the critical environmental problems we have are either caused or made much worse by the workings of our economic system. Even such issues as population growth and technology are best viewed in terms of their relation to the socioeconomic organization of society. It is true that competition and the drive for profits causes many companies to cut corners regarding worker and environmental safety—that's the reason strong regulations are needed (and they, of course, must be enforced). However, the overarching environmental problems are not a result of human ignorance or innate greed. They do not arise because the owners of businesses are morally deficient, although some clearly are. Nor is it simply due to lack of proper regulations. Instead, we must look to the fundamental workings of the political economy for explanations. It is precisely because ecological destruction is built into the inner nature and logic of our present system of production and distribution that it is so difficult to end.

Take world population growth, something many environmentalists consider a significant problem. Some promote zero population growth, while others say that the population must be drastically reduced from current levels. Today, as noted, the world's population is about seven billion people. Without a massive effort to change the current rate of increase, and absent an unprecedented catastrophe, demographers assure us that current trends indicate that global population will reach around 9 billion by midcentury and plateau at around 10 billion by the end of the century—a view that may prove overly optimistic.[9]

What is not always realized is that population growth cannot be examined apart from the economic system in which it is embedded. Negative or zero population growth can pose serious problems for a capitalist society always in search of new markets for its goods and requiring a continual expansion of the labor force and of the relative surplus population of the unemployed in order to meet the needs of production and profits. It is the existence of such a reserve army of the unemployed that holds down workers' wages, generating profits for those on the receiving end of the system.

When there is no population growth, there is little demand for new housing, severely affecting the construction industry. Fewer new households mean less purchasing of furniture and appliances. Without internal population growth, the push for external markets for sales becomes more critical for companies, and this can generate a variety of economic and political difficulties.

Another potential issue arising from low or no population growth in a capitalist economy is that there are fewer workers to support basic services for an aging population. Japan's population growth rate declined to around zero in 2005 and its population is projected to decline after 2010. Japan's declining population and the consequence that there are fewer workers have already created a host of problems for the country and forced it to begin importing workers from abroad—especially from the Philippines and Indonesia. According to the *Washington Post*, "For Japan, maintaining economic relevance in the next decades hinges on its ability—and its willingness—to grow [its population] by seeking outside help."[10]

There is no doubt that more people—all other things being equal—will put more stress on the environment. On the other hand, there is the issue of the standard of living of such a large number of people, as well as how production and living are organized. If a system can be brought about that promotes equality and aims to supply basic needs for everyone, it is more than conceivable that this could be done in an environmentally sound manner, even for nine billion people. On the other hand, if a substantial portion of the world's population, say a third or more, lives a commodity-intensive, high-consumption existence on the model of the United States, with all that such a mode of existence entails—private automobiles (and more than one per family), large houses, many televisions per house, new gadgets, luxury clothing, and the like—the ecological devastation of the planet is the most likely result. Herman Daly, as we noted in our Preface, calls the notion that the whole world can attain U.S. levels of per capita production and consumption the "Impossibility Theorem" since it would require as many as six planet Earths.[11] The solution is not to prevent poor countries from developing, but rather to insist that the rich countries move away from a system geared to profit, accumulation, and exponential economic growth, and toward a steady-state economy. And as the poor countries do develop they will need to aim at eventually achieving a sustainable economy.

Stephen Pacala, director of the Princeton Environmental Institute, illustrates this issue of world disparities in ecological footprints in relation to greenhouse gas emissions:

> The 3 billion poorest people . . . emit essentially nothing. The take-home message here is that you could increase the emissions of all of those people by putting diesel generators or anything you wanted into their lives and it would not materially affect anything I'm going to say. . . . In other words, the development of the desperately poor is not in conflict with solving the climate problem, which is a problem of the very rich. This is very, very important to understand. . . .

In contrast, the rich are really spectacular emitters. . . . the top 500 million people [about 8 percent of humanity] emit half the greenhouse emissions. These people are really rich by global standards. Every single one of them earns more than the average American and they also occur in all the countries of the world. There are Chinese and Americans and Europeans and Japanese and Indians all in this group.[12]

If growth of the economy and population clearly represent added burdens on the planet, technology is often seen as the silver bullet, which makes all things possible. But what technology, employed where, for what purpose? As Herman Daly has written:

The assumption of some critics [of the need to limit growth] that technology is exclusively a part of the solution and no part of the problem is ridiculous on the face of it and was totally demolished by the work of Barry Commoner [in *The Closing Circle*] (1971). We need not accept Commoner's extreme emphasis on the importance of the problem-causing nature of post–World War II technology (with the consequent downplaying of the roles of population and affluence) in order to recognize that recent technological change has been more a part of the problem than of the solution.[13]

Where technology is concerned, capitalism is far from neutral. It invariably favors those particular technologies that enlarge profits, accumulation, and economic growth. Indeed, it has a history of promoting those technologies that are most destructive of the environment: fossil fuel dependency, toxic synthetic chemicals (arising in particular from petrochemical production), nuclear energy, large dams, etc. In its headlong rush to expand, capitalism systematically gives rise to technologies that produce waste in vast quantities—as long as the costs can be externalized on nature and society and not on corporations themselves. Given that the technological objective is to feed growth, the tendency is to choose those technologies that maximize the overall through-put of resources and energy in the interest of higher overall economic output.

As Donella Meadows and her co-authors point out in *The Limits to Growth: The 30-Year Update*:

> If a society's implicit goals are to exploit nature, enrich the elites, and ignore the long term, then that society will develop technologies and markets that destroy the environment, widen the gap between rich and poor, and optimize for short-term gains. In short, that society develops technologies and markets that hasten a collapse instead of preventing it.[14]

Inequality as Usual

It is important to recognize that this is a question of class and other forms of social inequality, as well as inequality between nations. In 2008, Americans in the highest income quintile (the top 20 percent) spent three to four times as much on housing and clothing, and five times as much on transportation as those in the poorest quintile. In Canada, where consumption data is available by groupings that represent 10 percent of the population (deciles), ecological footprint analysts have found that the top income decile has an ecological footprint nine times that of the bottom decile, and a consumer goods footprint four times that of the bottom decile.

All such statistics, however, are invariably distorted by not including the super-rich as a separate statistical sample (and indeed their exclusion from the surveys altogether).[15] The income of the top 1 percent in the United States in 2006 (just prior to the Great Financial Crisis) was 21 percent of the total national income, about the same amount as the bottom 50 percent of the population.

Assuming that this income is all spent in one way or another on environmental consumption (equal to consumption plus investment in economic accounts), the average ecological footprint of those in the top 1 percent of income earners far exceeds that of those in the bottom half of the income distribution.[16]

This kind of inequality—which gives the rich and the super-rich in a country such as the United States ecological footprints sometimes a hundred or a thousand times more than those at the bottom—is only magnified at the global level. It is in fact the drive for greater, and more disproportionate, income and wealth on the part of those at the top of the system by means of ever-greater capital accumulation that keeps the entire economy going under capitalism. To reach a steady-state economy therefore requires going against not only power and wealth, but against the basic logic of capitalism as a system.

We shall argue in what follows that "solutions" proposed for environmental devastation (including zero population growth and new technology, however miraculous) that would allow the current system of production and distribution to proceed unabated are not real solutions. Indeed, such false solutions will in some ways make things worse by giving the impression that the problems are on their way to being overcome when the reality is quite different. The overwhelming environmental problems facing the world and its people will not effectively be dealt with until we establish another way for humans to interact with nature—altering not only the priorities of an economy but also the way decisions are made on what and how much to produce. Our most necessary, most rational goals require fulfilling basic human needs and creating sustainable conditions for present and future generations.

In order to map out the path to a real solution to the environmental and social problems that confront us, it is necessary to understand more fully why "business as usual," as defined by capitalism, makes the journey to a sustainable society impossible.

But the development of such an understanding of the limits of the present system is not enough. We must also recognize what has to be done in order to surmount the economic and social order in which we live—and what a truly just and sustainable society might look like.

3. The Growth Imperative of Capitalism

It is this obsession with capital accumulation that distinguishes capitalism from the simple system for satisfying human needs it is portrayed as in mainstream economic theory. And a system driven by capital accumulation is one that never stands still, one that is forever changing, adopting new and discarding old methods of production and distribution, opening up new territories, subjecting to its purposes societies too weak to protect themselves. Caught up in this process of restless innovation and expansion, the system rides roughshod over even its own beneficiaries if they get in its way or fall by the roadside. As far as the natural environment is concerned, capitalism perceives it not as something to be cherished and enjoyed but as a means to the paramount ends of profit-making and still more capital accumulation.

—PAUL M. SWEEZY[1]

The economic system that dominates nearly all corners of the world is capitalism. For most of us, capitalism is so much a part of our lives that it is invisible, like the air we breathe. We are as oblivious of it as fish are oblivious of the water in which they swim. It is capitalism's ethic, outlook, and internal values that we assimilate and acculturate to as we grow up. Unconsciously, we learn that greed, exploitation of laborers, and competition (among people, businesses, countries) are not only acceptable but are actually good for society because they help to make our economy function "efficiently."

Most of us are so enmeshed in capitalism that we are barely aware of it. It therefore requires some kind of rudimentary definition. A full definition of such a complex system would of course take volumes. Karl Marx wrote three volumes in defining capital as a social relation, and intended to write as many more.

In the briefest possible terms, capitalism is an economic and social system in which the owners of capital (or capitalists) appropriate the surplus product generated by the direct producers (or workers), leading to the accumulation of capital—investment and amassing of wealth—by the owners. Production takes the material form of the production of commodities for a market with the aim of generating profit and promoting accumulation. Individuals in this system pursue their self-interest, checked only by their mutual competition and by the impersonal forces of the market.

"Accumulate! Accumulate! That is Moses and the prophets" is the mantra of the system as a whole, as well as for each individual capitalist. The logic of accumulation and competition drives "bourgeois production out of its old course and . . . compels capital to intensify the productive forces of labour." It gives "capital no rest, and continually whispers in its ear: Go on! Go on!"[2] The resulting juggernaut accepts no boundaries to its expansion but continually tries to break them down, developing new technologies and expanding into new markets. Although this has at times paved the way to considerable social progress, the emphasis on accumulation for its own sake, which constitutes the inner logic of capital, carries heavy social and environmental costs, such as: (1) the polarization of income and wealth; (2) a continually large (if fluctuating) reserve army of the unemployed and underemployed; (3) periodic devastating economic crises; (4) an "externalization" of enormous costs on society and the environment; (5) systematic war and imperialism; and (6) the crippling of the potential of innumerable individuals.

The essence of capitalism, as described here, can be captured by rewording the First Commandment of the Bible as follows: "Thou shalt have no other gods before the accumulation of capital." Ecologist Richard Levins gives a concrete example of what this means: "Agriculture is not about producing food but about profit. Food is a side effect. . . . Health service is a commodity, health a by-product."[3] Although markets existed long before capitalism, an economy organized entirely around the production of commodities for sale for profit in a market, is unique to capitalism. Markets have become the almost universal places for obtaining goods and services. Capitalism, in this sense, can be seen as a system of generalized commodity production. Market sales and competitive conditions provide the "cues" to companies as to what to invest in, how much to produce, and whether to try to take over or outcompete a competitor—all for the purpose of maximizing profits. But the essence of the system lies not in such market relations, but in its exploitative relations of production. It is here that workers in effect rent out their capacity to work to the highest bidder, providing the surplus labor that forms the basis of profits under capitalism, and hence the foundation of the entire system.

Although capitalism's champions claim that the egoism that drives the system makes it maximally efficient and eminently fair, this is manifestly untrue. Capitalism is unplanned and anarchic, at one point resembling a drifting boat, at another a runaway train. Social regulations and controls are at a minimum. Inevitably, many unintended consequences occur in the production and distribution of goods and services. Mainstream economists call these "externalities"; to them, they are side effects of an otherwise rational and socially benign system. They include pollution of water, air, and soil, as well as disparities of wealth, significant periods of high unemployment, and failure to meet the basic needs of all people. They occur because they are excluded from the structure of economic costs and profits of the system, although they represent social and environmental costs. As economist K. William Kapp once observed,

> Generally speaking, capitalism must be regarded as an economy of unpaid costs, 'unpaid' insofar as a substantial portion of the actual costs of production remain unaccounted for in entrepreneurial outlays; instead they are shifted to, and ultimately borne by, third persons or the community as a whole.[4]

Let's take the example of coal to illustrate the significance of externalities. Coal is the cheapest fossil fuel when expressed as dollars per amount of energy obtained—the cost to electric generating plants in mid-2010 was less than $3 per million BTU for coal versus around $5 for natural gas and $16 for oil. In 2007 about 70 percent of the electricity generated by fossil fuels in the United States came from coal (coal generates about half of the electricity from all sources, including nuclear, hydro, etc.). *However*, the cost paid for coal does not include the ecological damage done when mining the coal (how could you even begin to calculate the cost of destroying a mountaintop and filling in the valleys?), the cost of lives lost in mining and of health effects (especially black lung disease) later in life, the cost of the mercury pollution of our lakes and the ocean—the cost of the contamination of fish and humans by that mercury, the greater acidity of the oceans, runoff from waste coal storage, the global warming effects of the carbon dioxide released into the atmosphere and methane released during mining, and so on. Though electric companies can be forced to shoulder some direct pollution costs (such as sulfur removal from coal smoke), the price paid in money for generating electricity from coal can never come anywhere near the full cost of the damage done to the earth and its inhabitants.

Let's consider some of the key aspects of capitalism's conflict with environmental sustainability. In doing so, keep two things in mind. First, the moving and motivating force of capitalism is the never-ending quest for profits and accumulation; and second, because of competition, companies are impelled continually to increase sales and to try to gain market share. In this chapter we will concentrate on the system's drive for private riches and its need to expand in order to avoid economic crises. The implications for the environment of this systemic drive to accumulate as well as other aspects of capitalism will be discussed in chapter 4.

Capitalist Economies Must Continually Expand

We are told all the time that only economic growth can make life better. But as Gus Speth tells us in the environmental journal *Solutions*:

> Economic growth may be the world's secular religion, but for much of the world it is a god that is failing—underperforming for most of the world's people and, for those in affluent societies, now creating more problems than it is solving. The never-ending drive to grow the overall U.S. economy undermines communities and the environment. It fuels a ruthless international search for energy and other resources; it fails at generating the needed jobs; and it rests on a manufactured consumerism that is not meeting the deepest human needs. Americans are substituting growth and consumption for dealing with the real issues—for doing things that would truly make the country better off. Psychologists have pointed out, for example, that while economic output per person in the United States has risen sharply in recent decades, there has been no increase in life satisfaction, and levels of distrust and depression have increased substantially.[5]

The failing god of growth that Speth describes for the United States is nothing more than the way capitalism operates at its most basic level. No-growth capitalism is an oxymoron: when accumulation ceases, the system is in a state of crisis, with considerable suffering for the working class. Capitalism's motive force is the competitive amassing of profits for new capital formation in order to generate more profits and accumulation, *ad infinitum*. This leads to exponential or compounded economic growth. As the authors of *The Limits to Growth* wrote:

> Much of each year's output is consumable goods, such as textiles, automobiles, and houses, that leave the industrial system. But some fraction of the production is more capital—looms, steel mills, lathes—which is an investment to increase the capital stock. Here we have another feedback loop [in addition to population growth]. More capital creates more output, some variable fraction of the output is investment, and more investment means more capital. The new, larger capital stock generates even more output, and so on.[6]

Nothing could be more opposed to capitalism as a system than the commonplace depiction of it in terms of a simple exchange process in which a commodity (C) is exchanged for money (M) to purchase another commodity (C), so that the process ends with a definite use value that is simply consumed, or C–M–C. This is similar to barter (C–C), but with money used as an intermediary instead of directly exchanging one product for another. In such an exchange process there is a definite end, with the consumption of the commodity, which becomes the whole object and consummation of the process.

But as economists from Karl Marx to John Maynard Keynes pointed out this is a false picture. Rather, the general formula of exchange under the capitalist system of production actually takes the more dynamic form of M–C–M′, in which money is used to purchase the inputs to produce a commodity, which is then sold for

more money or M´ (M + Δm). The object, in other words, is to end
up with *more money* than one started with, that is, surplus value or
profits. Such an exchange process has no end, but simply goes on
and on without limit. Thus in the next round exchange takes the
form of M´–C–M´´, which leads in the round after that to
M´´–C–M´´´, and so on in an incessant drive to accumulation at
ever higher levels.[7]

Capital, understood in this way, is self-expanding value.
Capitalism thus recognizes no limits to its own self-expansion—
there is no amount of profit, no amount of wealth, and no amount
of consumption that is either "enough" or "too much." This
means that the environment exists, not as a place with inherent
boundaries within which human beings must live together with
Earth's other species, but as a realm to be exploited in a process
of growing economic expansion. Businesses, according to the
inner logic of capital, which is enforced by competition, must
either grow or die—as must the system itself.

The trend toward ever-greater concentration of capital is built
into the whole process of capital accumulation. When a new
product is first produced, or a new industry arises, there may be
many producers. But as the industry matures a few firms come to
dominate the market. In general, size wins out, with bigger capi-
tals beating and absorbing smaller ones. Of course, there are always
many small businesses, especially in local markets—restaurants,
barbershops, plumbing and electrical contractors—where a long-
term niche is developed and the owners are content not to
expand. Small companies do provide employment—with some
13 million U.S. jobs in 2008 in firms with fewer than ten employees. The small business sector, however, generally represents a
low- profit, non-expansive, part of the economy, which has relatively little impact on the economy as a whole, and accounts for
only a very small part of value added. Moreover, as the Center for
Economic Policy and Research declared in its 2009 report, *An
International Comparison of Small Business Employment*: "By

every measure of small business employment, the United States has among the world's *smallest* small-business sectors (as a proportion of total employment)."[8]

The representative firm in today's economy is rather a giant monopolistic/oligopolistic corporation, which is both a conglomerate and a multinational firm. For such firms the imperative is to grow larger to take advantage of economies of scale. Competition occurs primarily through cost-reduction and the sales effort rather than lowering prices, while there is a constant push to buy other companies. In this sector, which dominates the modern economy, a corporation that does not grow and increase its market share will indeed die.

Examples abound of companies whose founders either had a social mission or originally wanted to remain small but were ultimately forced to accept the reality of competition in the marketplace. For example, a number of food-related companies such as Ben & Jerry's (ice cream), Whole Foods Markets (originally a small natural foods store in Austin, Texas), and Green Mountain Coffee Roasters (a company that views "profit as a means of achieving a higher purpose to do good for others around the world")[9] were either sold to a larger company that had a better chance of propelling growth (such as Ben & Jerry's, acquired by Unilever) or managed to buy out their competitors as part of their growth strategy.

Over a period of one year, Green Mountain Coffee Roasters purchased three companies: Diedrich Coffee Inc., Timothy's Coffees of the World Inc., and Van Houtte, based in Canada. The company's CEO explained the last of these as follows: "This acquisition will enhance Green Mountain's Canadian presence and is expected to strengthen our North American geographic expansion with a well-known Canadian brand platform that includes roasting, manufacturing and distribution capabilities."[10]

Whole Foods explains the expansion of its "natural foods" empire in similar terms:

Beginning in 1984, Whole Foods Market began its expansion out of Austin, first to Houston and Dallas and then into New Orleans with the purchase of Whole Food Company in 1988. In 1989, we expanded to the West Coast with a store in Palo Alto, California. While continuing to open new stores from the ground up, we fueled rapid growth by acquiring other natural foods chains throughout the 90s: Wellspring Grocery of North Carolina, Bread & Circus of Massachusetts and Rhode Island, Mrs. Gooch's Natural Foods Markets of Los Angeles, Bread of Life of Northern California, Fresh Fields Markets on the East Coast and in the Midwest, Florida Bread of Life stores, Detroit area Merchant of Vino stores, and Nature's Heartland of Boston.[11]

Donald R. Knauss, chairman and CEO of Clorox—makers of everything from bleach to Brita water-filtration systems, and Glad bags, wraps and containers—explained his company's takeover of Burt's Bees and its line of green-friendly products:

This acquisition allows us to enter a growing market that's consistent with consumer megatrends. . . . With this transaction, we're entering into a new strategic phase for our company, enabling us to expand further into the natural/sustainable business platform. The Burt's Bees® brand is well-anchored in sustainability and health and wellness, and we believe it will benefit from natural and "green" tailwinds. It's in an economically attractive category with a margin structure that will be highly accretive to Clorox. Combined with our new Green Works™ line of natural cleaning products, and Brita® water-filtration products, we can leverage Burt's Bees' extensive capabilities and credibility to build a robust, higher-growth platform for Clorox.[12]

In the same press release Clorox's Vice President for Strategy & Growth added: "We strongly believe Clorox's deep capabilities to drive demand creation through consumer communication and value-creating customer capabilities, coupled with Burt's Bees' strong heritage of innovation to delight consumers, create a right to win."

Such mergers and acquisitions, through which small, innovative, and socially concerned companies are bought out in the end by large corporations that respond only to the demands of their owners for higher profits, enhanced stockholder equity, and increased firm size are the rule in today's capitalist economy. In 2007 worldwide mergers and acquisitions reached a record $4.38 trillion, up 21 percent from 2006.[13]

Monopoly and Competition

The end result of competition between firms, which leads to the concentration and centralization of production both nationally and internationally, is that a relatively small number of firms end up controlling large segments of the market in mature industries and are able to exert near-monopoly control. Once just a few oligopolistic firms control 50 percent or more of a market, competition in the classic sense is replaced by what Joseph Schumpeter called "corespective" behavior, in which price competition is increasingly curtailed.[14] Such firms tend effectively to ban price cutting, while increasing prices only in tandem (often following the lead of the largest firm). In 1947 the largest four firms already accounted for 50 percent or more of the value of shipments in 31 percent of all industry groupings in U.S. manufacturing. However, by 2007 this had risen eight percentage points with the top four firms accounting for 50 percent or more of shipment value in 39 percent of all manufacturing industry groupings.[15] The last two decades have seen rapid concentration in nearly every major sector of industry, including manufacturing, retail, and finance.[16]

Such consolidation of industry is often touted as promoting more efficiency and having beneficial "trickle-down" effects for the general public. However, as a *New York Times* editorial pointed out:

> The supposed consumer benefits are often unconvincing. Pennzoil's acquisition of Quaker State led to more expensive motor oil, Procter & Gamble's purchase of Tambrands led to more expensive tampons, and General Mills' purchase of the Chex brands led to more expensive cereal, according to one study. Despite limits imposed by antitrust regulators, the merger between Guinness and Grand Metropolitan to create the food and drink giant Diageo led to substantial increases in the price of Scotch.[17]

Although corporations in mature, capitalist economies, dominated by oligopolies, generally refrain from genuine price competition, which is frequently referred to pejoratively as price warfare, lowering prices is still used in some instances to try to gain (or maintain) market share. But as the CEO of the home products company Colgate-Palmolive said, "Pricing is often a nonsustainable answer."[18] Continual competition by trying to undercut the competition *is* unsustainable—the recipe for most companies to bleed themselves to death. As two Harvard Business School teachers and a corporate consultant explained in the *Wall Street Journal*, competing by lowering prices "definitely works for a few companies. But the reality is a very few—think Wal-Mart or Costco or Southwest Airlines. In fact, the very success of these business models makes it difficult for their competitors to duplicate—think Kmart or Sears, or any number of bankrupt budget airlines."[19] And once these price-cutters have gained sufficient market dominance, it is a good bet that their price cutting will come to an end.

Hence, one of the traits of a monopoly-capitalist economy, characterized by a high degree of concentration, is a structural shift from price competition to competition in other areas, particularly with respect to the sales effort or marketing in all of its forms (targeting, motivational research, product management, advertising, sales promotion, etc.). Such "monopolistic competition," as economists refer to it, has led in the last fifty years to an explosion in the rates of consumption linked to increasing wasteful lifestyles, often financed by growing household debt. We have changed almost every aspect of the way we eat, drink, travel, house ourselves, wash, rest, and play. In doing so, we have generally assumed that the resources and energy these activities rely on—energy from fossil fuels, in particular—are limitless and cheap, and their use free of serious consequences. Hence the ecological impact of the daily routines of millions of people across the world, who have bought into consumer capitalism, has increased like a slow-motion explosion.[20]

It would be wrong, however, mainly to fault the individual consumer. Under a mature, monopoly-capitalist system, people serve the economy and not vice versa. The much ballyhooed "consumer sovereignty" is transformed, as John Kenneth Galbraith pointed out, into "producer sovereignty."[21] Consumers are viewed as mere actors to be manipulated by those who write the scripts. The massive and, in Schumpeter's words, "elaborate psychotechnics of advertising" are absolutely necessary to keep people buying.[22] Marketing consultant Victor Lebow saw this as early as 1955, when he wrote in the *Journal of Retailing*:

> Our enormously productive economy demands that we make consumption our way of life, that we convert the buying and use of goods into rituals, that we seek our spiritual satisfactions, our ego satisfactions, in consumption. The measure of social status, of social acceptance, of prestige, is now to be found in our consumptive patterns. The very meaning and significance of our lives is today expressed in consumptive terms. The greater the pressures upon the individual to conform to safe and accepted social standards, the more does he tend to express his aspirations and his individuality in terms of what he wears, drives, eats —his home, his car, his patterns of food serving, his hobbies.

These commodities and services must be offered to the consumer with a special urgency. We require not only "forced draft" consumption, but "expensive" consumption as well. We need things consumed, burned up, worn out, replaced, and discarded at an ever increasing pace. We need to have people eat, drink, dress, ride, live, with ever more complicated and, therefore, constantly more expensive consumption. The home power tools and the whole "do-it-yourself" movement are excellent examples of "expensive" consumption.

What becomes clear is that from the larger viewpoint of our economy, the total effect of all the advertising and promotion and selling is to create and maintain the multiplicity and intensity of wants that are the spur to the standard of living in the United States. A specific advertising and promotional campaign, for a particular product at a particular time, has no automatic guarantee of success, yet it may contribute to the general pressure by which wants are stimulated and maintained. Thus its very failure may serve to fertilize this soil, as does so much else that seems to go down the drain.

As we examine the concept of consumer loyalty, we see that the whole problem of molding the American mind is involved here.[23]

The stimulation of consumption takes many forms. Advertisements in newspapers, magazines, free-standing ads, billboards, radio, television, and on the web continually confront people with subtle and not-so-subtle pushes to consume. Companies also bring out "new and better" models of their products—cell phones, computers, cars—in a bid to grab attention and convince people that they need the latest version. One type of competition in the effort to stimulate sales and consumption is to have more and more products at consumers' fingertips—in 2009 the average supermarket in the United States had an almost unbelievable 48,000 items on its shelves.[24] However, these products are increasingly provided by a relatively small number of firms.

Whole aisles in a supermarket are taken up by soft drinks provided mainly by just two firms: Coke and Pepsi.

Most advertising can only be viewed as parasitic and without social value. Consider the "battles" between companies producing razors for shaving—especially Gillette (a $4-billion-a-year company) and Schick ($1 billion). The razor wars for increased sales and market share have had companies going from single-edge razors to double to four and five blades. Gillette now promotes "its Fusion ProGlide's ergonomic grips, its ultrafine cutting edge and a 'snow-plow guard' that moves around the shaving cream. It goes for $16.99 per four-pack of basic cartridges, about a 15% premium to regular Fusion blades." On the other hand, a "four-pack of blades for Schick's new Hydro—with a hydrating 'reservoir'—runs $11.49, about 5% more than Schick's premium Quattro blades." As one frustrated buyer put it, "It's easier to buy uranium. . . . They're so expensive they have to keep them locked up, and that's when I realized what a gimmick all of it is."[25] Another example is the "diaper war," with companies engaged in monopolistic competition by coming up, for example, with different "designer" disposable diapers as a way to gain market share. It is not uncommon for advertising alone, apart form other marketing expenditures, to account for 11 or 12 percent of the store price of certain products, such as toothpaste, soap, or men's jeans.[26]

Some television networks are even using being "green" as a marketing tool—and advertisers are responding. New behavioral placement ads are viewed as an advance on standard "product placement," where a particular product is used as a prop in a show. In the case of behavioral placement, viewers are encouraged "to adopt actions they see modeled in their favorite shows. For example, actors are shown using water coolers rather than plastic water bottles in the office (a behavior promoted by sellers of office water coolers). In 2007 NBC launched "Green Week," the behavioral programming component of a wider "Green Is Universal" corporate campaign. As a result it was able to pull in an estimated $20 million in advertising revenue from 20 sponsors.[27]

The newest marketing push has been through the mediums of the Internet and cell phones. AT&T is getting customers to sign up for its new marketing program ShopAlerts™, allowing it to direct location-based marketing at individuals using the GPS tracking installed on their cell phones. In this way AT&T is selling ads to companies, such as SC Johnson, Hewlett Packard, and Kmart, which helped to launch ShopAlerts. Text-message ads are being sent by AT&T to cell phone owners whenever they enter particular "geo-fences."[28]

Other companies are tracking everything that people do on the Internet and then creating a profile of the person—guessing age, sex, purchasing preferences, car owned, income, and the like, based on the individual's Internet activity. These companies then sell the information to other companies that use it to target ads specifically to the individual. When a person visits Capital One's credit card page, the company uses a program devised by the firm called [x+1]. "In a fifth of a second, [x+1] says it can access and analyze thousands of pieces of information about a single user. It quickly scans for similar types of Capital One customers to make an educated guess about which credit cards to show the visitor." Better deals are offered for people with "better" profiles.[29]

Companies are always seeking out new frontiers for their products. Two of the most recent forays into new areas of marketing involve the beginning of life and the end of life. The Walt Disney Company is giving away a free "Disney Cuddly Bodysuit" for babies soon after birth. "In bedside demonstrations, the bilingual representatives extol the product's bells and whistles—extra soft! durable! better sizing!—and ask mothers to sign up for e-mail alerts from DisneyBaby.com."[30] Apparel is viewed as only the "beachhead"—Disney estimates the North American market for baby products including infant formula is about $36 billion annually. Robert A. Iger, chief executive of Disney, explained in a giddy fashion: "If ever there was an opportunity for a trusted brand to enter a market and provide a better product and experience, it's this. . . . I'm extremely excited about it."[31]

And as the baby boomers hit sixty-five, other companies are salivating over the potential of marketing to them as well as to aging people in other countries. As Eric Dishman, the global director of health innovation at Intel, put it: "There is an enormous market opportunity to deliver technology and services that allow for wellness and prevention and lifestyle enhancement. . . . Whichever countries or companies are at the forefront of that are going to own the category."[32]

After dealing with infants and the aged, can't you just imagine the new underserved demographic segments—maybe the "preborn" and those in the afterlife?

According to Blackfriars Communications, the United States in 2005 spent over $1 trillion on marketing in its various forms—representing about 9 percent of U.S. GDP. Retail industry was found to spend 12 percent of its revenue on advertising.[33] In comparison, total spending on elementary and secondary education in the United States in 2004–05 was $536 billion, or only a little more than half of marketing expenditures.[34]

The emphasis on consumption has even brought about a change in everyday language use. Instead of talking about the "people," the "general population," the "public," or "humanity," it is common to use the term "consumer." But what does it mean to refer to "consumer spending," a "consumer advocate," or the "food consumer"? Since everyone needs to consume food, this is really a reference to all of humanity. "Consumer demand" is another way of expressing either a need of people or an artificially created want—*as long as it translates into new purchases*. A *Wall Street Journal* article titled "Consumers Tighten Belts" tells how people in the United States are cutting back on spending in the aftermath of the Great Recession.[35] Of course, people consume things just as fish or cows or elephants do. But is the key characteristic of other animals (or plants, for that matter), their consumption? As people are converted into "consumers" in common speech and in the media—with the emphasis placed on their ability to purchase and consume—we have lost the essence of our common humanity. Our humanity is being defined as our connection to commodities instead of to each other and our communities.

The Growth Problem
of Mature Capitalist Economies

Although capitalist economies are impelled toward growth, relatively slow growth seems to be the baseline (or default setting) for mature capitalist countries. Why does this occur, how do capitalists deal with this, and what are the consequences for working people?

When a relatively small number of firms dominate a market, the power that gives them over both workers and the general public raises profit margins, generating a high and rising volume of profits. Thus, the top 200 U.S. corporations saw their gross profits as a percentage of total business profits in the U.S. economy rise from 13 percent in 1950 to over 30 percent in 2007.[36] However, for such giant firms and the economy to continue to grow, these enormous profits must find profitable future outlets within production or the "real economy." That is, the demand for goods and services must continue to increase.

Problems arise, however, on a number of fronts. First, when companies are very large and dominant in a market, they do not always make proportionately large capital expenditures, even if new technologies are available. This is partly because their existing capital was expensive, and they want to fully depreciate it (use it up to the maximum extent possible) before scrapping it. This tends to slow down capital spending—what economists call investment—and thereby slow the growth of the economy.

Second, monopoly power gives businesses great leverage over workers, who, unless they are well organized, find their wages stagnating. This in turn restricts demand for consumer goods, and again tends to slow the growth of the economy. Third, investment is hindered by the large quantities of unused productive capacity (both intended and unintended) under capitalism with a high degree of economic concentration. Firms are reluctant to invest in new productive capacity if a considerable portion of their existing capacity is standing idle. Indeed, industries that are run on a monopolistic or quasi-monopolistic basis are careful to regulate and restrict the expansion of their productive capacity in order to maintain higher prices and profits. Finally, mature industries in which productive capacity has been built up over the years are less dynamic in investment terms than new industries in which demand is being built up from scratch. The more developed economies, in which mature industries predominate, therefore tend to be less dynamic overall.

There are ways that the economy may still grow rapidly, despite the tendency toward slow growth, since they are seen as threats to the private market. A revolutionary innovation such as the automobile might come along and spur massive capital spending. A war might spur growth. The government might tax unspent profits and invest the tax revenues itself in, for example, public works projects, and this can get the economy growing rapidly again. However, none of these things can be depended upon, and employers will vigorously oppose unions and new government spending as a means of stimulating growth since they are seen as threatening to the private market.

It is true that the system can continue to move forward, to some extent, as a result of financial speculation leveraged by growing debt, even in the face of a tendency to slow growth in the underlying economy. This is what happened in the United States in the years before the Great Recession. Lacking profitable outlets for investment within production, corporations decided to open financial divisions and poured whatever surplus they gained from production into speculation of various kinds in the financial system. The automobile industry was in trouble long before the Great Recession. During some of this period, GM was losing money when selling cars, but the company actually made money because of the profits from the financial division, GMAC. During this period GM was leveraged to the hilt and brought to the brink of bankruptcy when the financial crisis hit in 2007.

At the same time, consumers used their credit cards and borrowed against rising home values to sustain their standards of living in the face of thirty years of stagnant wages. The result was rapidly rising household debt, which helped fuel the financial bubble, and led to record mortgage defaults once the bubble burst.

Financial bubbles, as we have seen again and again in the history of capitalism, and more frequently in the current period of monopoly-finance capital, serve to lift the economy—until they inevitably burst.[37] The question then becomes the distribution of the losses, which fall primarily on those without economic and political power.

Financial expansion in our time has become a means of leveraging a stagnant economy, and creating a modicum of economic growth—at all times a necessity for capitalism. But the dire consequences that such enormously distorted, wasteful, and parasitic processes have for the population in general and the environment are incalculable.

Is Zero Growth Capitalism Possible?

Although mature capitalist countries are plagued by the tendency toward stagnation, these economies do generally continue to grow. So let us return again to the argument that economic growth has to be slowed down even more or stopped altogether if we are to have any chance of creating a sustainable environment. Is this even possible in a capitalist economy? One might imagine that it is theoretically possible for a capitalist economy to have zero growth and still meet all of humanity's basic needs.[38] Let's suppose that all the profits that corporations earn (after allowing for replacing or repairing worn-out equipment and buildings) are either spent by capitalists on their own consumption or given to workers as wages and benefits, and consumed. As capitalists and workers spend this money, they would purchase the goods and services produced, and the economy could stay at a steady state, no-growth level (what Marx called "simple reproduction" and which has sometimes been called the "stationary state"). Since there would be no investment in new productive capacity (beyond replacement), there would be no economic growth, no additional profits generated. In other words, there would be no capital accumulation.

There is, however, a central problem with this "capitalist no-growth utopia": it violates the basic motive force of capitalism. What capital strives for—the purpose of its existence—is its own expansion. Why would capitalists, who in every fiber of their beings believe that they have a personal right to business profits, and who are driven by competition to accumulate wealth, simply turn around and spend the economic surplus at their disposal on their own consumption or (less likely still) give it to workers to spend on theirs—rather than seek to expand wealth? On the contrary, it is clear that owners of capital will, as long as such ownership relations remain, do whatever they can within their power to maximize the amount of profits they accrue. A stationary state, or steady-state, capitalist economy is only conceivable if separated from the reality of the social, economic, and power relations of capitalism itself.

Capitalism is a system that constantly generates a reserve of unemployed workers. Full employment is a rarity that occurs only at very high rates of growth, which are correspondingly dangerous to ecological sustainability. As Christina Romer, former chair

Table 1. Change in Unemployment at Different Growth Rates of the Economy, 1949–2008

PERCENT CHANGE IN REAL GDP FROM PREVIOUS YEAR	AVERAGE PERCENT CHANGE IN UNEMPLOYMENT FROM PREVIOUS YEAR*	NUMBER OF YEARS	YEARS WITH GROWTH IN UNEMPLOYMENT
<1.1	1.75	11	11
1.2–3.0	0.13	13	9
3.1–5.0	−0.25	23	3
>5.0	−1.02	13	0

*A negative number indicates a growth in employment.
Source: NIPA Table 1.1.1. Percent Change from Preceding Period in Real Gross Domestic Product; Series Id: LNS14000000, Current Population Survey, Bureau of Labor Statistics, Quarterly Unemployment Rate.

of President Obama's Council of Economic Advisers, tells us, "We need 2.5 percent growth just to keep the unemployment rate where it is. . . . If you want to get it down quickly, you need substantially stronger growth than that."[39]

Taking the U.S. economy as the example, let's take a look at what happens to the number of "officially" unemployed when the economy grows at different rates during a period of close to sixty years (see Table 1). For background, we should note that the U.S. population is growing by a little less than 1 percent a year, as is the normal working-age population (new entrants to the labor force minus those that are above normal working age). In U.S. unemployment measurements, those considered to be *officially unemployed* must have looked for work within the last four weeks and cannot be employed in part-time jobs. In contrast, individuals without jobs, who have not looked for work during the previous four weeks (but who have looked within the last year), either because they believe there are no jobs available, or because they think there are none for which they are qualified, are classified as *discouraged* and are not counted as officially unemployed. Other *marginally attached workers*, who have not recently looked for work (but have in the last year), not because they were "discouraged," but for other reasons, such as lack of affordable day care, are also excluded from the official unemployment count. In addition, *those working part-time but wanting to work full-time* are not considered to be officially unemployed. The unemployment rate for the more expanded definition of unemployment (U-6) provided by the Bureau of Labor Statistics includes the above categories (discouraged workers, marginally attached workers, and part-time workers desiring full-time employment) and is generally almost twice the official U.S. unemployment rate (U-3). In the following analysis, however, we focus only on the official unemployment data.

What, then, do we see in the relationship between economic growth and unemployment over the last six decades?

- During the eleven years of very slow growth, less than 1.1 percent per year, unemployment increased in each of the years.

- In 70 percent (nine of thirteen) of the years when GDP grew between 1.2 and 3 percent per year, unemployment also grew.

- During the twenty-three years when the U.S. economy grew fairly rapidly (from 3.1 to 5.0 percent a year), unemployment still increased in three years and reduction in the percent unemployed was anemic in most of the others.

- Only in the thirteen years when the GDP grew at greater than 5.0 percent annually did unemployment not increase in any of these years.

Although Table 1 is based on calendar years and does not follow business cycles, which of course do not correspond neatly to the calendar, it is clear that if the GDP growth rate isn't substantially greater than the increase in the working population, people lose jobs. While slow or no growth is a problem for business owners trying to increase their profits, it is a disaster for working people.

What this tells us is that the capitalist system is not very efficient at creating jobs relative to its economy's ability to grow. As mentioned in a *Washington Post* article, "A growth rate in the mid-2 percent range signifies an economy merely treading water. Population growth and technological improvement mean that the United States is capable of increasing its economic output by 2.5 to 3 percent per year indefinitely, so growth faster than that is needed to bring down joblessness and put idle factories to use."[40] It will take a prolonged period in which the rate of growth is around 4 percent or higher, far above the average growth rate, before the U.S. unemployment problem is surmounted.

Worth noting is that since the 1940s such high rates of growth in the U.S. economy have hardly ever been reached except in times of war. Real full employment last happened in the United States during the Second World War when some 16 million men were in the armed forces and there was an all-out production for the war effort under government financing. The wars in Iraq and Afghanistan, while certainly supplying a stimulus to the United States economy, do not have anything close to the effect of the Second World War (or even the Korean and Vietnam wars). There are now far fewer people in the armed forces and the war machine is highly mechanized, thus employing fewer people. (There was a short period of relatively high GDP growth in the bubble-expanding mid to late 1990s. Although it was based on a huge expansion of debt and speculation, the higher growth rate during that period did reduce unemployment.)

The Paradox of Growth

The growth imperative is a basic characteristic of individual firms as well as the capitalist system as a whole, derived from the accumulation of capital. Companies that do not grow are in precarious situations, and may not survive. Growth for the economy as a whole—significantly higher than the rate of population increase—is required, as we have seen, in order to provide enough jobs to keep unemployment from destabilizing the society. Extreme hardships develop for workers when corporations or the economy as a whole do not grow for a number of quarters of a year—or even if the economy grows slowly for a prolonged period.

As shown by the Great Recession and its aftermath, capital is generally not hurt as much in a downturn as workers are. Indeed, owners have ways of sticking workers with the costs of an economic crisis or stagnation. Today the recession is technically over and profits soaring, yet the economy remains stagnant, with the masses of workers forced to make up for the relative losses associated with the slow growth of the system. In such circumstances, what economists call a zero-sum game applies, and profits come at the direct expense of wage income. Put simply: if the overall economic pie is not growing, or is growing very slowly, it is still possible for those with power to get much bigger slices, but only by dishing out diminished portions to everyone else.

In general, environmental quality improves during recessions, with fewer emissions from smokestacks and discharges into water, fewer miles driven by the public, and less natural resource mining. However, one of the ways in which the system tries to revitalize capital accumulation and growth under such conditions is by removing protections for the environment, which are considered an unaffordable luxury in hard economic times. Insofar as this helps the capitalist economy recover, however, it is often doubly destructive of the environment: since not only have environmental protections been relaxed to spur growth, but the expanding economy now draws on more energy and resources.

4. The Environment and Capitalism

Since there is no way to increase the capacity of the environment to bear the burdens placed on it [by population and the economy], it follows that the adjustment must come entirely from the other side of the equation. And since the disequilibrium has already reached dangerous proportions, it also follows that what is essential for success is a reversal, not merely a slowing down, of the underlying trends of the last few centuries.

—PAUL M. SWEEZY[1]

Given the growth juggernaut that characterizes capitalism, the system is most destructive toward the environment when it is working well and economic growth rates are high. It is least environmentally destructive when the system is in economic crisis and growth is faltering. When the economy is in recession and production and transportation are decreased, the air tends to be less polluted; less CO_2 is produced from fossil fuels; fewer minerals are extracted, and so on. Recessions, then, are good for the environment. However, recessions cause tremendous suffering for many people. In the current period, beginning with the Great Recession and extending into the weak and uneven recovery, it is not only the millions of unemployed and their families that suffer. Many of the employed have been forced to work fewer hours, take a pay cut or unpaid leave, and pay more for their health insurance.

In the midst of the 2010 Gulf of Mexico oil-discharge disaster workers in the region were pitted against government agencies that wanted a moratorium on new deep-water drilling until safety mechanisms could be reassessed and strengthened. This is not the only time the environment and labor have seemed to be in opposite camps (for example, the decrease in clear-cutting of old-growth forests in the Pacific Northwest to try to save the endangered spotted owl pitted environmentalists against loggers), and it underscores that in this economic system people are forced to take the jobs capitalists choose to provide. This frequently places the need for jobs in opposition to the need for a clean environment, sometimes causing internal conflicts in the minds of workers. As a retired coal miner said regarding mountaintop removal, "I know it put bread on my table, but I hate destroying the mountains like that."[2] Labor environmentalists often refer to the unacceptable choice that workers are given between jobs and the environment as the "job blackmail."[3] In periods of recession this job blackmail becomes more severe, opening the way to expansion in production and employment by the removal of environmental safeguards.

In chapter 3 we discussed the imperative to grow that is central to capitalist economies, together with the tendency in mature capitalist economies to slow growth—even economic stagnation. Such a slowdown means a reduction in the rate of growth of demands on the environment. Nevertheless, this is not as good for the environment as one might think, since the amount of growth can still be substantial given that we are dealing with such large economies. Therefore, even the generally slower growth of mature economies is far too much for the environment to sustain. In addition, when a country like the United States is able to import much more than it exports, the environmental effects of production in countries such as China, Vietnam, India, or Bangladesh for the U.S. market need to be added to the U.S. environmental balance sheet.

Now let's take a look at the concrete implications of the drive to perpetual growth—including how it affects people's outlook and the behavior of business and government with respect to the environment.

The Global Race for Raw Materials, Cheaper Labor, and New Markets

As companies expand, they begin to saturate the home market and look abroad for new markets to sell their goods. For example, as a report for the U.S. Grocery Manufacturers Association put it: "The case for global expansion is quite simple. As domestic markets are saturated, global expansion is one way to achieve sustainable, double-digit growth."[4] Despite difficulties, retail giant Wal-Mart is persisting in its penetration into India "because its effort in India is critical to its global growth strategy. Confronted with saturated markets in the United States and other developed countries, the company needs to establish a bigger presence in emerging markets, like India, where modern stores make up just 5 percent of the country's retail industry."[5] Wal-Mart's international sales are now growing "almost nine times the rate of domestic sales."[6] Looking for foreign markets is also critical for European companies. Carrefour, the French corporate inventor of huge hypermarkets, has run into the same problem of "sluggish consumer spending in its home market . . . [and] has rolled out hypermarkets in booming new consumer markets such as China and Brazil."[7]

In the United States, it's not just Wal-Mart that is going abroad in a chase for ever-increasing profits—a decade ago the foreign sales of the Standard and Poor's 500 corporations accounted for 20 percent of total corporate revenue, and now supply approximately 30 percent of income.[8] Total U.S. corporate profits from activities abroad were around 6 percent in the 1960s but exceeded a quarter of total profits in 2008.[9] In addition to expanding markets abroad, corporations and their governments (working on behalf of corporate interests) help to secure entry and control over key natural resources such as oil and a variety of minerals.

One outcome of the recent globalization of capital and the specter of global food shortages is a massive landgrab. Private capital and government sovereign wealth funds (state-managed investment funds, often under the control of a central bank) are striving to gain control of vast acreage throughout the world to produce food and biofuel feedstock crops for their home markets. It is estimated that some 30 million hectares of land (roughly equal to two-thirds of the arable land in Europe), much of it in Africa, has been recently acquired or is in the process of being acquired by foreign countries and international corporations.[10] This global land seizure (even if by "legal" means) can be regarded as part of the larger history of imperialism.

Today, multinational corporations scour the world for resources and opportunities wherever they can find them, exploiting cheap labor, taking advantage of lax environmental regulations, and relying on tax benefits in poor countries. All of this reinforces, rather than reduces, divisions among the wealthy countries and poor countries. The result is a more rapacious global exploitation of nature and increased differentials of wealth and power. Such global corporations have no loyalty to anything but their own bottom lines. Despite rapid income growth in some countries, primarily in Asia, inequality between the poorest and richest countries of the world persists and for much of the world has deepened. The gap between the richest and poorest regions of the world rose in the last quarter of the twentieth century from 13:1 to 19:1. From 1970 to 1989 the annual per capita GDP of the developing countries (excluding China) averaged a mere 6.1 percent of the per capita GDP of the G7 countries (the United States, Japan, Germany, France, the United Kingdom, Italy, and Canada). From 1990 to 2006 (just prior to the Great Financial Crisis) this dropped to 5.6 percent. Meanwhile, the average GDP per capita of the forty-eight or so Least Developed Countries (a UN-designated subset of developing countries) as a share of average G7 GDP per capita declined from 1.4 percent in 1970–1989 to .96 percent in 1990-2006.[11]

The story of centuries of European and U.S. plunder and expansion is well documented.[12] Sometimes economic penetration of the poorer nations of the global South occurred peacefully while in many cases warfare was needed in order to gain domination. The U.S.-led wars in Iraq and Afghanistan follow the same general historical pattern of colonial and imperial powers exerting their influence, and are clearly related to U.S. attempts to control the main world sources of oil and gas, as well as show the world the extent of U.S. military might and its willingness to use it.[13]

China, a rapidly growing economic power, increasingly integrated into the world capitalist economy, is searching the world for investment opportunities in raw materials and is starting to build up its navy to protect shipping lanes, especially for oil from the Persian Gulf. China is in effect simply attempting to survive like any other major economy in the global capitalist system, but its outward expansion is being treated as aggression by the established imperial powers and being used as a justification for their own renewed scramble for resources in the Central Asia, the Persian Gulf, and West Africa. The result is a growing intensification of world geopolitical struggles.[14]

In his great work *The Power Elite* sociologist C. Wright Mills spoke of a "military metaphysics," whereby all world problems are turned into military problems, requiring military solutions. There is no doubt that the growing economic demands of capitalist economies in an age of "generalized monopoly capital" increasingly transform issues of economic globalization into issues of geopolitics in which the military becomes more and more prominent, threatening world stability and even survival.[15]

If society doesn't change, we can only look forward to enhanced strife among the wealthy nations for the resources of the South, more direct conflict between China and the already wealthy countries (especially the United States), as well as more civil wars in the poor but resource-rich countries where the income from the exports goes to the powerful and already wealthy.

Resource competition is causing growing environmental conflict. For example, disputes among countries over water are intensifying. The long-standing Pakistan-India dispute is partially over water. Despite a treaty on water use between the two countries, India's use of the waters in the six rivers that flow from the Indian Punjab and Indian-controlled Kashmir, and its planned new water diversions, has Pakistan concerned about the cumulative effects of these actions on water flow into its territory. And in the Middle East, the presence of productive aquifers in the Palestinian West Bank region is one of the many reasons that Israel has not wanted to give up the territory to a Palestinian state. China's dams on a number of rivers that flow into Indochina have that region's nations worried over reduced flows during key times of the year.

Ecological and Resource Limits

The irreversible exhaustion of finite natural resources will leave future generations without the possibility of using them. Natural resources are used in the process of production—oil, gas, and coal for fuel; water in industry and agriculture; trees for lumber and paper; a variety of mineral deposits, such as iron ore, copper, and bauxite in manufacturing; and so on. Liquid fossil fuels form the basis of the world's transportation systems—automobiles, buses, trains, trucks, ships, and airplanes. Some resources, such as forests and fisheries, are of a finite size but can be renewed by natural processes if used in a planned system that is flexible enough to change as conditions warrant. Future use of other resources—oil and gas, minerals, and aquifers in some desert or dryland areas (prehistorically deposited water)—are limited forever to the supply that currently exists. The water, air, and soil of the biosphere can continue to function well for the living creatures on the planet only if pollution doesn't exceed their limited capacity to assimilate and render the pollutants harmless.

Business owners and managers generally consider only the short term in their operations. Most take into account the coming three to five years, or, in some rare instances, up to ten years. This is the way they *must* function because of unpredictable business conditions (phases of the business cycle, competition from other corporations, prices of needed inputs such as raw materials, and investors not wanting to wait too long for profits) and demands from speculators looking for short-term returns. They therefore act in ways that largely ignore the natural limits to their activities—as if there were an unlimited supply of natural resources for exploitation. Even if the reality of environmental limitation enters their consciousness, it merely speeds up the exploitation of a given resource, which is extracted as rapidly as possible, with capital then moving on to new areas of resource exploitation. With each individual capitalist pursuing the self-interested goal of making a profit and accumulating capital, decisions are made that collectively harm society.

The length of time before nonrenewable deposits are exhausted depends on their size and rate of extraction. Whereas depletion of some resources may be hundreds of years away (assuming that the rate of growth of extraction remains the same), decreased availability for some important ones—oil and some minerals—are not that far off. For example, even if we use the conservative estimates of the oil companies, at the rate at which oil is currently being consumed known crude oil reserves will be exhausted within the next fifty years and peak production will be reached within a couple of decades. The prospect of peak oil is projected in numerous corporate, government, and scientific reports. The question today is not whether peak oil is likely to arrive soon, but simply how soon.[16] In order to compensate for the peaking of low-cost crude oil, companies are resorting to very environmentally damaging production of oil from tar sands of Canada and oil and gas from shale deposits of Texas and other parts of the United States.

Although oil may be one of the most discussed non-renewable resources facing depletion, it is far from the only one. For example, the known deposits of the critical fertilizer ingredient phosphorus will be exhausted in this century, even if usage doesn't grow.[17] This is because of the rupture of the traditional cycling of nutrients from crops and animals to people and back to farmland—the metabolic rift discussed about a century and a half ago by Karl Marx: "Capitalist production collects the population together in great centres, and causes the urban population to achieve an ever-growing preponderance. . . . It disturbs the metabolic interaction between man and the earth, i.e. it prevents the return to the soil of its constituent elements consumed by man in the form of food and clothing; hence it hinders the operation of the eternal natural condition for the lasting fertility of the soil."[18]

Faced with limited natural resources, there is no rational way to prioritize usage under a modern capitalist system, in which the better-off, with their economic leverage, decide via their purchasing power and investment decisions how commodities are to be allocated. When extraction begins to decline, as is projected for crude oil within the next few decades, price increases will put more pressure on what was, until recently, the boast of world capitalism: the supposedly well-off "middle-class" in the rich ("developed") countries. The capitalist rush to own and use global resources is compounded by government support for private companies, such as the enormous tax breaks handed out to U.S. oil companies, amounting to billions of dollars a year.

Added to this, particularly in the United States, is the military's resource race. As stated in the *Wall Street Journal*,

> The U.S. military is gearing up to become a more active player in the global scramble for raw materials, as competition from China and other countries raises concerns about the cost and availability of resources deemed vital to national security. The Defense Department holds in government warehouses a limited number of critical materials—such as cobalt, tin and zinc—worth about $1.6 billion as of late 2008.[19]

The well-documented decline of many ocean fish species, almost to the point of extinction, is an example of how even "renewable resources" can be exhausted. It is estimated that one-third of commercial fisheries are producing at only 10 percent of their onetime potential as a result of overfishing and that nearly all commercial species will be in that category by midcentury.[20] It is in the short-term interests of the individual owners of fishing boats—some of which operate at factory scale, catching, processing, and freezing fish—to maximize the take. Hence, the fish are rapidly depleted.

The depletion of fish off the coast of Somalia because of overfishing by fleets composed of factory-scale ships is believed to be one of the causes for the rise of piracy that now plagues international shipping in the area. Interestingly, the neighboring Kenyan fishing industry is rebounding because the pirates also serve to keep large fishing fleets out of the area.

In addition to overfishing, pollution and acidification are decreasing the productivity of the oceans. And the fish that are caught are polluted with by-products of industry such as mercury that goes up the smokestacks of coal-burning electric-generating plants.

No one protects the common interest. In a system driven by private self-interest and accumulation, the state is normally incapable of helping to manage the resource until a catastrophe has already occurred. This relates to the well-known "tragedy of the commons," whereby resources belonging to all are systematically plundered by private interests. Indeed, it is not the existence of the commons itself that is at fault here, but the fact that under a capitalist system public wealth is often left unprotected and robbed for individual gain, as opposed to being sustainably managed as a shared heritage. Hence, we should properly refer to *the tragedy of the private exploitation of the commons.*

The situation is very different when communities that have a stake in the continued availability of a resource consciously manage it in place of private firms. Genuine communities are organized around the common or communal interest. In contrast, corporations are subject to the Hobbesian world of the war of all against all. Theirs is a single-minded goal of maximizing short-term profits— after which they move on, leaving environmental devastation behind. There is no natural limit to human greed, which is to a large extent stimulated by social conventions and mores. However, there are limits, as we are daily learning, to many resources, including "renewable" ones, such as the productivity of the seas.

The exploitation of renewable resources before they can be renewed is referred to as "overshooting" the resource. This is occurring not only with the major fisheries but also with groundwater. As water is pumped faster than recharge, water tables are falling in the area of the Oglala aquifer in the Great Plains of the United States, large areas of northwestern India, northeast Pakistan, North Africa, and northeast China. The enormous amount of water being pumped from aquifers—mainly to irrigate crops—is having a significant effect on the global hydrologic cycle. "People are drawing so much water from below [ground] that they are adding enough of it to the ocean (mainly by evaporation, then precipitation) to account for about 25 percent of the annual sea level rise across the planet."[21]

Overshoot is also occurring with tropical forests in South America and Southeast Asia as well as in Africa. Duke University ecologist John Terborgh described a trip he took to a small African nation where foreign economic exploitation is combined with a ruthless depletion of resources:

> Everywhere I went, foreign commercial interests were exploiting resources after signing contracts with the autocratic government. Prodigious logs, four and five feet in diameter, were coming out of the virgin forest, oil and natural gas were being exported from the coastal region, offshore fishing rights had been sold to foreign interests, and exploration for oil and minerals was under way in the interior. The exploitation of resources in North America during the five-hundred-year post-discovery era followed a typical sequence—fish, furs, game, timber, farming virgin soils—but because of the hugely expanded scale of today's economy and the availability of myriad sophisticated technologies, exploitation of all the resources in poor developing countries now goes on at the same time. In a few years, the resources of this African country and others like it will be sucked dry. And what then? The people there are currently enjoying an illusion of prosperity, but it is only an illusion, for they are not preparing themselves for anything else. And neither are we.[22]

Wendell Berry describes the environmental and human disaster of the United States coal industry, most recently exemplified by mountaintop removal in order to reach the coal:

> For more than 100 years the coal-producing counties of eastern Kentucky have been dependent on the coal industry, which has dominated them politically and, submitting only to the limits of technology, has come near to ruining them. The legacy of the coal economy in the Kentucky mountains will be immense and lasting damage to the land and to the people. Much of the dam-

age to the land and the streams, and to water quality down-
stream, will be irreparable within historical time. . . . The coal
economy . . . has been an *imposed* economy, coming in from the
outside and also coming down from the high perches of wealth
and power. It is the product of an abstracting industrial and mer-
cenary intelligence, alien both to the nature of the land and to the
minds and lives of the people.[23]

Berry is describing, without using the word *capitalism*, how
the capitalist system naturally functions. It's nothing particularly
new or unusual. In the 1880s, Frederick Engels explained how
capitalism leads to environmental disasters:

As individual capitalists are engaged in production and exchange
for the sake of the immediate profit, only the nearest, most immediate results must first be taken into account. As long as the individual manufacturer or merchant sells a manufactured or purchased commodity with the usual coveted profit, he is satisfied
and does not concern himself with what afterwards becomes of
the commodity and its purchasers. The same thing applies to the
natural effects of the same actions. What cared the Spanish
planters in Cuba, who burned down forests on the slopes of the
mountains and obtained from the ashes sufficient fertilizer for *one*
generation of very highly profitable coffee trees—what cared they
that the heavy tropical rainfall afterwards washed away the unprotected upper stratum of the soil, leaving behind only bare rock! In
relation to nature, as to society, the present mode of production is
predominantly concerned only about the immediate, the most
tangible result; and then surprise is expressed that the more
remote effects of actions directed to this end turn out to be quite
different, are mostly quite the opposite in character.[24]

The 2010 oil disaster in the Gulf of Mexico, which cost eleven
workers their lives and resulted in major and long-lasting ecological

damage to the Gulf and the ecologically and economically important wetlands, put a spotlight on BP, formerly British Petroleum. BP is a company that has cut corners in the search for more profits as shown by: the 2006 Alaska oil pipeline spill; the March 2005 Texas refinery explosion that killed fifteen people and injured 170 others; and the 2010 release of significant quantities of pollutants, including about 17,000 pounds of benzene, a known carcinogen, by the same Texas refinery that exploded in 2005.

One of the responses to the 2010 BP oil discharge in the Gulf of Mexico—estimated at close to five million barrels (one barrel of oil is equivalent to 42 gallons or 160 liters)—was the use of massive quantities of "dispersants" which work like a detergent to help break up masses of oil and thus assist in the breakdown of oil by microorganisms. The material, Corexit (or a variation of it), contains known toxic agents, and the U.S. Environmental Protection Agency said that it should be used only in "rare cases." It was sprayed on surface oil, as well as near the ocean floor at the point of oil discharge. The material was used a total of seventy-four times on fifty-four different days, with as much as 10,000 gallons (approximately 40,000 liters) used in a day.[25]

The Gulf of Mexico has long been a sink that receives pollutants from U.S. industry and agriculture, most transported by the Mississippi River. And though BP may be an especially troublesome or rogue corporation with regard to worker safety and the environment, the net effect of the oil industry—including those corporations with better safety and environmental records—was harmful to the Gulf and the wetlands well before 2010. Loss of wetlands from Louisiana's coastal region, estimated at some 100 km² per year, is caused by many factors, including the channeling (and constructed levees) of the Mississippi River and sea-level rise. However, the canals dug through the wetlands to lay pipelines and to reach drilling rigs produced a landscape riddled with interconnecting canals that are 2.5 meters deep and some up to a thousand meters long. These canals allow easy access for saltwater and storm surges, which are responsible for a significant percent of wetland losses. "The wildlife-rich coastal wetlands of Louisiana, sliced up and drastically engineered for oil and gas exploration, shipping and flood control, have lost an area larger than Delaware since 1930."[26]

In addition to the disturbances that assist wetland destruction, there are 27,000 abandoned oil and gas wells in the Gulf, some neglected since the 1940s—"an environmental minefield that has been ignored for decades."[27] Because abandoned wells on land frequently leak, it is safe to assume that there are leaking abandoned wells in the Gulf, many of which were plugged "temporarily" or with outdated procedures. And in fact, there have been many oil spills in the Gulf before the BP spill in 2010—amounting to an estimated 517,000 barrels between 1964 and 2009, equivalent to twice as much as leaked from the *Exxon Valdez* in 1989.[28]

With both companies and governments pushing more and more growth and as the easily exploitable resources are exhausted, increased environmental ruin is inevitable. As the easily recoverable (and cheap) oil and gas are already being utilized, deposits that are more difficult to reach or extract are utilized. Thus we see deep-ocean drilling for oil, the extraction of oil from tar sands, and hydraulic fracturing ("fracking") of shale deposits (using toxic chemicals mixed with water, to access trapped natural gas and oil), all of which have been demonstrated to have the potential to cause extreme environmental harm. For example, oil extraction from the Canadian tar sands uses about four gallons of water to produce every gallon of oil, consumes about 20 percent of Canada's production of relatively clean natural gas, strips forests off the land, leaves massive "ponds" filled with toxic residue throughout the region of extraction, and "produces 82% more greenhouse-gas emissions than does the average barrel refined in the U.S."[29]

New York Times columnist Bob Herbert summed up the danger to our environment posed by the control of a resource as important as oil by transnational oil companies:

How is it possible for anyone with any reasonable awareness of the nonstop carnage that has accompanied the entire history of giant corporations to believe that the oil companies, which are among the most rapacious players on the planet, somehow "had their act together" with regard to worst-case scenarios?

These are not Little Lord Fauntleroys who can be trusted to abide by some fanciful honor system. These are greedy merchant armies drilling blindly at depths a mile and more beneath the seas while at the same time doing all they can to stifle the government oversight that is necessary to protect human lives and preserve the integrity of the environment.

President Obama knows that. He knows—or should know—that the biggest, most powerful companies do not have the best interests of the American people in mind when they are closing in on the kinds of profits that ancient kingdoms could only envy. BP's profits are counted in the billions annually. They are like stacks and stacks of gold glittering beneath a brilliant sun. You don't want to know what people will do for that kind of money.[30]

As bad as the environmental destruction caused by capitalist enterprises in the United States is, the situation in poor countries is even worse. For example, the environmental and human problems in Nigeria's Niger delta because of oil extraction by Western oil companies far exceeds damage caused by the 2010 oil discharge in the Gulf of Mexico. Author and activist Ken Saro-Wiwa was executed in 1995 by the Nigerian government because of his environmental activism on behalf of his Ogoni people and against the pollution and corruption of the oil companies, dominated by Shell. He described this region as "a blighted countryside . . . full of carbon dioxide, carbon monoxide and hydrocarbons; a land in which wildlife is unknown; a land of polluted streams and creeks, of rivers without fish." Or, as he put it in a poem:

The flares of Shell are flames of hell
We bake beneath their light
Nought for us save the blight
Of cursed neglect and cursed Shell.[31]

Soils that used to grow food and fiber are being degraded through widespread abuse, threatening the ability to feed the world's people. Erosion—accelerated greatly by intensive tillage and resulting in the loss of fertile topsoil—and decreased organic matter (caused by tillage and by lack of sufficient return of residues) reduce soil biodiversity, nutrient availability, and water-holding capacity, leading to lower crop production.

Many temperate region forests were cut down during the pre- and early-industrial ages. Tropical forests in South America, Africa, and Southeast Asia are now being lost at a rapid pace—decreasing earth's biodiversity, displacing indigenous peoples, and interfering with the water cycle.

Human production not only runs up against the limits of resources but even more the limits of the extent to which the environment can absorb the wastes generated and the rifts in ecological cycles that this creates. The result of all of this is widespread ecological degradation. This can be seen, as we have already noted, in the crossing of planetary boundaries. Natural sources of nitrogen fixation—conversion of the atmospheric N_2 gas into forms that can be used by plants—have been critical to the development and maintenance of life on Earth. The overuse of industrial production of nitrogen fertilizers adds significantly to the amount of "fixed" nitrogen in soils, causing increased pollution of ground and surface waters with nitrates and increased N_2O (a potent greenhouse gas) emissions to the atmosphere. "Agricultural soil management activities such as fertilizer application and other cropping practices were the largest sources of U.S. N_2O emissions in 2008."[32] Leaching of nitrates resulting from excess use of nitrogen fertilizers and lack of ecologically sound rotations is one of the main causes of the hundreds of "dead zones" of low oxygen coastal areas of oceans around the world.

More and more of the terrestrial (land-based) photosynthesis of plants is now directly used by humans, accounting for upwards of 40 percent of the total.[33] All ecosystems on Earth are in visible decline. With the increasing scale of the world economy, the human-generated rifts in the Earth's metabolism inevitably become more numerous and severe. Yet the demand for more and greater economic growth and accumulation is built into the capitalist system, leading to ever worsening environmental conditions with respect to the planet as a whole.

Capitalist Ideology and Mores

Capitalism leads to a loss of connection with nature, fellow humans, and community. The self-centered and consumer culture fostered by the system (see below) means that people lose close connections with nature—which is seen predominantly as a source of materials for enhancing the exploitation of other people and other communities.

This severing of connections with nature may be one of the reasons why people in wealthy countries report that they are less happy with each passing decade. Apparently quite a few people are at least aware of the problem. The difficult times of the Great Recession and the period of high unemployment coupled with deteriorating environmental conditions have negatively affected families, creating desires for another way of living:

A craving for a simpler, slower, more centered life, one less consumed by the soul-emptying crush of getting and spending, runs deep within our culture right now. It was born of the boom, and not just because of the materialism of that era but also because of the work it took then to keep a family afloat, at a time of rising home prices and health care costs, frozen real wages and the pressures of an ever-widening income gap. As the recent Rockefeller report showed, for most families the miseries of the Great Recession don't represent a break from the recent past, just a significant worsening of the stresses they've been under for years and years.[34]

The reciprocity that was present in farming communities in the United States still exists in small pockets. It was once common for people to ask neighbors for help or to borrow something without any expectation about future give and take. Nobody kept score as various types of assistance went back and forth—using gravel from a neighbor for your field road, bringing a tractor to get a neighbor's equipment out of the mud, milking cows for a neighbor when tragedy struck the family. Some reciprocity continues in rural areas, and it can even be found in cities. But today it is more common in large cities, and even in some rural areas, to not even know your neighbors well or think of asking them for help when you might need it.

Ideologically, capitalism is based on the proposition that each, following his/her own interests (greed), will promote the general interest and growth. Adam Smith famously put it: "It is not from the benevolence of the butcher, the brewer, or the baker, that we expect our dinner, but from their regard to their own interest."[35] In other words, individual greed drives the system and human needs are satisfied as a mere by-product. Economist Duncan Foley has called this Smithian proposition and the economic and social irrationalities it generates "Adam's Fallacy."[36] "If we continue to act on the assumption that the only thing that matters is personal greed and personal gain," Noam Chomsky has stated, "the [ecological] commons will be destroyed. Other human values have to be expressed if future generations are going to be able to survive."[37]

The attitudes and mores needed for the smooth functioning of such a system, as well as for individuals to thrive in such an acquisitive society—greed, individualism, competitiveness, exploitation of others, and consumerism—are constantly inculcated into people by schools, the media, and the workplace. The title of Benjamin Barber's book—*Consumed: How Markets Corrupt Children, Infantilize Adults, and Swallow Citizens Whole*—says a lot.[38] Contrast this emphasis on competition and consumerism with the words of Albert Einstein: "This crippling of individuals I consider the worst evil of capitalism. Our whole educational system suffers from this evil. An exaggerated competitive attitude is inculcated into the student, who is trained to worship acquisitive success as a preparation for his future career."[39]

The notion of responsibility to others and to community erodes under such a system. In the words of Gordon Gekko—the fictional corporate takeover artist in Oliver Stone's film *Wall Street*—"Greed is good." Today, in the wake of widespread public outrage, with financial capital walking off with big bonuses derived from government bailouts, capitalists have turned to preaching self-interest as the bedrock of society from the very pulpits. On November 4, 2009, Barclay's PLC CEO John Varley declared from a wooden lectern in St. Martin-in-the-Fields in London's Trafalgar Square: "Profit is not Satanic." Weeks earlier, on October 20, 2009, Goldman Sachs International advisor Brian Griffiths declared before the congregation at St. Paul's Cathedral in London, "The injunction of Jesus to love others as ourselves is a recognition of self-interest."[40] As a Yale law professor explained in the summer of 2009, "High profits are excellent news. When corporate earnings reach record levels, we should be celebrating. The only way a firm can make money is to sell people what they want at a price they are willing to pay. If a firm makes lots of money, lots of people are getting what they want."[41] The law professor seems oblivious to the fact that so many profits are gained by a variety of financial gimmicks and gambling—usually referred to as speculation—that nothing whatsoever of value to anyone is produced except the money that accrues to those who win the bets. He, of course, also completely ignores that the system constantly creates in people the desire to consume and, contrary to evidence, to believe that more and more consumption will make them happier.

Wealthy people have come to believe that they deserve their wealth because of hard work, either theirs or their forebears. The ways in which their wealth and prosperity arose out of the social labor of innumerable other people are denied. They see the poor—and the poor, taught to be self-denigrating, frequently agree—as having something wrong with them, such as laziness or not getting a sufficient education. The structural obstacles that prevent most people from significantly bettering their conditions are ignored or downplayed. This view of each individual as a separate economic entity concerned primarily with his/her own well-being (extending at most to one's immediate family), obscures our common humanity and needs.

Selfishness, one of many human traits, does not inherently overwhelmingly influence our actions. U.S. sociologist and economist Thorstein Veblen wrote, in the early twentieth century, of fundamental social drives such as the "parental bent" and the "instinct of workmanship" that accounted for the creativity and cooperation of human beings as one side of our character.[42] However, selfishness is actively promoted in present-day society in response to the pressures and underlying logic of the capitalist system. After all, if each person doesn't look out for "Number One" in a dog-eat-dog system, who will? Matters are even more serious when the future of humanity is concerned. In a society that emphasizes grabbing everything one can immediately, the needs of future generations are frequently left out of account altogether.

Traits fostered by capitalism are commonly viewed as being innate to "human nature," thus making a society organized around goals other than the profit motive unthinkable. But humans are clearly capable of embracing a wide range of characteristics, extending from great cruelty to great sacrifice for a cause, to true altruism. The "killer instinct" we supposedly inherited from evolutionary ancestors—the evidence being chimpanzees killing the babies of other chimps—is being questioned by reference to the peaceful characteristics of other hominids such as gorillas and bonobos (as closely related to humans as chimpanzees).[43] Studies of human babies have also shown that, though selfishness is a human trait, so are cooperation, empathy, altruism, and helpfulness.[44] Wisdom teaches us, as Einstein emphasized, that human beings are both solitary and social beings. To emphasize the former at the expense of the latter is to invite destruction.[45]

Regardless of what traits we may have inherited from our hominid ancestors, research on precapitalist societies and history indicate that very different norms from those in capitalist societies were encouraged and expressed. Following his first voyage to the so-called New World, Columbus indicated he had not "been able to learn whether they held personal property, for it seemed to me that whatever one had, they all took shares of. . . . They are so ingenuous and free with all they have that no one would believe it who has not seen it; of anything they possess, if it be asked of them, they never say no; on the contrary, they invite you to share it and show as much love as if their hearts went with it." Commenting on this, William Brandon, a prominent historian of American Indians, stated:

> Many travelers in the heart of America, the Indian world real before their eyes, echoed such sentiments year after year, generation after generation. These include observers of the most responsible sort, the missionary Du Tertre for a random example, writing from the Caribbean in the 1650s: ". . . they are all equal, without anyone recognizing any sort of superiority or any sort of servitude. . . . Neither is richer or poorer than his companion and all unanimously limit their desires to that which is useful

and precisely necessary, and are contemptuous of all other things, superfluous things, as not being worthy to be possessed."[46]

Economic anthropologist Karl Polanyi summarized the numerous studies on pre-capitalist societies as follows: "The outstanding discovery of . . . historical and anthropological research is that man's economy, as a rule, is submerged in his social relationships. He does not act so as to safeguard his individual interest in the possession of material goods; he acts so as to safeguard his social standing, his social claims, his social assets."[47]

These pre-capitalist societies were certainly not perfect. There were local tyrants and wars and other such occurrences. But they are proof that differently organized societies have encouraged the expression of different traits than those promoted by capitalism. In his 1937 article on "Human Nature" for the *Encyclopedia of the Social Sciences*, John Dewey concluded—in terms that have been verified by all subsequent social science—that

the present controversies between those who assert the essential fixity of human nature and those who believe in a greater measure of modifiability center chiefly around the future of war and the future of a competitive economic system motivated by private profit. It is justifiable to say without dogmatism that both anthropology and history give support to those who wish to change these institutions. It is demonstrable that many of the obstacles to change which have been attributed to human nature are in fact due to the inertia of institutions and to the voluntary desire of powerful classes to maintain the existing status.[48]

Capitalism is unique among social systems in its active, extreme cultivation of individual self-interest or "possessive individualism."[49] Yet the reality is that non-capitalist human societies have thrived over a long period—for more than 99 percent of the time since the emergence of anatomically modern humans—while encouraging other traits such as sharing and responsibility to the group, and respect for the environment. There is no reason to doubt that this can happen again.[50]

Environmental Degradation
Especially Hurts the Poor

Capitalism confers large rewards upon some fortunate individuals, while it condemns all too many less fortunate ones to the economic scrap heap. There is a logical connection between capitalism's successes and its failures. The poverty and misery of a large mass of the world's people is not an accident, some inadvertent by-product of the system, one that can be eliminated with a little tinkering here or there. The fabulous accumulation of wealth—as a direct consequence of the way capitalism works nationally and internationally—has simultaneously produced enormous poverty in such forms as: persistent hunger, malnutrition, health problems, lack of water, lack of sanitation, and general misery for a large portion of the people of the world. The wealthy few resort to the mythology that the grand disparities are actually necessary. For example, as Brian Griffiths, the previously mentioned advisor to Goldman Sachs International, put it: "We have to tolerate the inequality as a way to achieve greater prosperity and opportunity for all."[51] In this view, some of the increased wealth in the society will supposedly "trickle down" to those lower on the ladder, although how long this might take or how it will actually happen is never mentioned. Indeed, the system actually pumps wealth endlessly up to those at the top of society, who do their best to keep it coming at a faster and faster pace, while preventing any downward trickle.

Most people need to work in order to earn wages to purchase the necessities of life. But due to the way the system functions, large numbers of people are precariously connected to jobs. They are hired during times of growth and fired as growth slows or as their labor is no longer needed for other reasons— Marx, as we have noted, referred to this group as the "reserve army of labor."[52] This group of "disposable" workers—easily hired and easily fired—now contains people with significant skills, some of whom are trying to live a "middle-class" lifestyle. Given a system with booms and busts, one in which profits are the highest priority, it is not merely convenient to have a group of people in the reserve army, it is absolutely essential to the smooth workings of the economy. It serves, above all, to hold down wages and instill workplace discipline. Today the general law of accumulation that constantly reproduces this reserve army of labor operates on a global scale, with hundreds of millions of unemployed/underemployed.

In accordance with its underlying logic, then, the system produces a huge inequality of both income and wealth, which then passes from generation to generation. The production of great wealth and, at the same time, great poverty, within and between countries, is not coincidental—wealth and poverty are actually two sides of the same coin.

In 2007, the top 1 percent of wealth holders in the United States controlled 33.8 percent of the wealth of the country while the bottom 50 percent of the population owned a mere 2.5 percent. Indeed, the richest *400 individuals* had a combined net worth of $1.54 trillion in 2007—approaching that of the bottom *150 million people* (with an aggregate net worth of $1.6 trillion). On a global scale, the wealth of the world's 793 billionaires was, in 2008, more than $3 trillion—equivalent to about 5 percent of total world income ($60.3 trillion in 2008). A mere 2 percent of the world's adult individuals have more than half of the global household wealth, with the richest 1 percent accounting for 40 percent of total global assets; while the bottom half of the world's population has barely 1 percent.[53] As wealth becomes more concentrated, the wealthy gain more political power, and they do what they can to hold on to as much money as possible—at the expense of those in lower economic strata. Most of the productive forces of society, such as factories, machinery, raw materials, and land, are controlled by a relatively small percentage of the population.

The poor do not have access to good homes, environmentally safe neighborhoods, or adequate and healthy food supplies because they do not have "effective" demand—although they certainly have biologically based demands. All goods are commodities and as such are produced and made available only if there is an effective demand for them and if they generate profits for the sellers. People without sufficient money have no right in the capitalist system to any particular type of commodity— whether it is a luxury such as a diamond bracelet or a huge McMansion, or whether it is a necessity of life such as a healthy physical environment, reliable food supplies, clean drinking water, or quality medical care. Access to all commodities is determined not by desire or need, but by having the wherewithal to purchase them. Coupled with this is the fact that this is a system that by its very workings produces inequality and holds back workers' wages, ensuring that many (in some societies, most) will not have access even to the basic necessities or to what we might consider a decent human existence.

This segment of society, the poor, are produced and maintained in their low economic position by the very workings of capitalism. It's true that we are all harmed by polluted air, food, and water. That's why our bodies are contaminated with so many harmful chemicals. And climate change will affect us all to one degree or another. But wealthier people have more options to deal with these issues. They can eat organic food regularly and move to less polluted communities. They have access to the best of all of life's amenities. In contrast, it is the poor who are by far the most vulnerable to environmental degradation. Climate change has already hurt many poor people because of disappearing glaciers (loss of irrigation and drinking water), rising seas, and more extreme weather. The same is true for other types of environmental damage. A growing "environmental justice" movement has focused attention on the burden that environmental degradation places on poor communities in terms of toxic wastes in particular. Polluting industries and waste disposal facilities tend to be sited in poor neighborhoods or in unincorporated areas without zoning laws and with people who have few resources to fight back.

Mossville, Louisiana, is a textbook example of the toll that poor air quality and polluted water can take on a town situated next to industries that annually emit thousands of pounds of known carcinogens such as benzene and vinyl chloride.[54] A chemist working with Mossville's residents explains: "The people of Mossville are like an experiment. They know that they have high levels of dioxin in their blood, and they're allowed to continue to live there and be exposed." As Lisa Jackson, the head of the U.S. Environmental Protection Agency, said: "Historically, the low-income and minority communities that carry the greatest environmental burdens haven't had a voice in our policy development or rulemaking."[55] In response to this, EPA has released a document, "Interim Guidance on Considering Environmental Justice during the Development of an Action."[56] It remains to be seen how effective this effort will be in actually lessening the environmental hazards heaped on poor communities in the United States. And even if it is relatively effective, it's important to remember that it can always be overturned by a new administration.

Waste, including highly toxic industrial waste, is frequently exported to poor countries for disposal or supposed recycling. Beginning in the 1970s, African countries—such as Nigeria, Ghana, and Ivory Coast—have been prime recipients of the industrial and sewage wastes of developed countries. Larry Summers, a former top economic advisor to President Obama and former president of Harvard University, claimed, in a 1991 memo written when he was chief economist of the World Bank,

that "underpopulated countries in Africa are vastly *under*polluted, their air quality is probably vastly inefficiently low [sic]
compared to Los Angeles or Mexico City. Only the lamentable
facts that so much pollution is generated by non-tradable industries (transport, electrical generation) and that the unit transport
costs of solid waste are so high prevent world-welfare-enhancing
trade in air pollution and waste."[57] So there's a supposedly
rational economic reason to pollute poor countries. And because
of differences in power, little is done about purposeful pollution
by Western corporations—a Dutch court fined an oil trading
company, Trafigura, only one million euros (about $1.3 million)
for a 2006 incident of toxic sludge dumping in the Ivory Coast
that resulted in sixteen deaths and thousands of people becoming
ill.[58] Such meager fines, rather than constituting a deterrent, can
be factored in as a regular business expense in the process of generating profits.

The Business Cycle and the Environment

In the boom phase of the ordinary business cycle, factories and
entire industries produce more and more, while at the same time
expanding productive capacity (structures and equipment)
through new capital formation. Corporate owners and managers
assume that the boom will never end and, not wanting to miss out
on the "good times," end up producing too much and overbuild-
ing capacity in relation to effective demand. Since effective
demand is no longer sufficient to provide a market for all of the
goods produced and/or potentially produced, and to realize
anticipated profits, the business cycle enters its downward phase.
Realized profits (together with expectations of future profits)
decline, investment falters, and the economy sinks.

For these as well as other reasons the capitalist system is prone
to periodic crises of overaccumulation of capital during which the

poor and near-poor suffer the most. Recessions occur with some regularity, along with depressions, which are less frequent. As we write, we are in the aftermath of a deep recession or mini-depression (with 9 percent official unemployment in the United States in May 2011), and many think we averted a full-scale depression by the skin of our teeth. All told, since the mid-1850s there have been thirty-two recessions or depressions in the United States (not including the current one)—with the average contraction since 1945 lasting around ten months and the average expansion between contractions lasting about six years.[59] Ironically, from the ecological point of view, as we have noted, major recessions—although causing great harm to many people—are actually a benefit, since lower production leads to less pollution of the atmosphere, water, and land.

The Capitalist State and the Environment

One of the main roles of the state under capitalist economies is to assist business. Despite all the "free market" and "free trade" rhetoric we hear, governments of all the wealthy nations give strong assistance to help their corporations grow, increase their exports, and expand abroad. Means of assistance to business include the following examples: colonial adventures, such as the British forcing the Chinese government to sign the 1842 Treaty of Nanking, which included eliminating protective tariffs that made the costs of imports from Britain and its colonies prohibitively high; U.S. imperial adventures, such as the 1953 overthrow of the Iranian government that resulted in significant U.S. corporate control of Iran's oil; assisting development of new technologies, as the U.S. government does through defense research and development; direct subsidies to industries, such as the oil industry and biofuel production; and so on. *New Yorker* economic columnist John Cassidy has explained: "The fact is that not one of today's economic powers practiced free trade during its developmental stage."[60]

President Obama in his January 2011 State of the Union Address to Congress made it clear that he wants the United States to be better able to compete with other countries: "We know what it takes to compete for the jobs and industries of our time. We need to out-innovate, out-educate, and out-build the rest of the world."[61] And he called for government investment to help this to occur. Though his new initiatives may not become reality—because of concern over government deficits and the ideological composition of members of Congress—he is only calling for more of the same in terms of the subsidizing of corporate research and development by government. "Because it's not always profitable for companies to invest in basic research," he pointed out, "throughout our history, our government has provided . . . the support that they need."[62]

The incestuous connection that exists today between business interests, politics, and law is reasonably apparent to most observers.[63] These range from outright bribery to the more subtle sorts of buying access, friendship, and influence through campaign contributions and lobbying efforts. As early twentieth-century humorist Will Rogers was fond of saying, "We have the best Congress that money can buy." This was never truer than it is today. In discussing an ethics inquiry directed at members of the U.S. Congress who took money from financial interests, a *New York Times* article began as follows:

> Lawmakers take contributions every day from corporate executives and lobbyists hoping for their votes. The question of whether that represents business as usual in Washington or an ethics breach is at the heart of a far-reaching Congressional ethics investigation that is stirring concerns throughout Washington and Wall Street.[64]

There has been much discussion but little done about the "revolving door" as people go from government to industry (or lobbying organizations) and sometimes back again to government. Three out of four oil and gas lobbyists in Washington in 2010 formerly worked for the federal government.[65] This creates an atmosphere in which government agencies don't properly enforce the regulations that exist—prime examples are in the off-shore drilling for oil and the coal industry—let alone request new regulations. In the process, Congress and government agencies are overwhelmingly influenced by—if not actually in the pockets of—industry.

The multibillionaire Koch brothers, who are heavily invested in the oil industry, have been instrumental in promoting doubt about the science of global warming. In her exposé of the role of the Koch brothers in creating a political environment hostile to environmental sanity, Jane Mayer wrote:

In a 2002 memo, the Republican political consultant Frank Luntz wrote that so long as "voters believe there is no consensus about global warming within the scientific community" the status quo would prevail. The key for opponents of environmental reform, he said, was to question the science—a public-relations strategy that the tobacco industry used effectively for years to forestall regulation. The Kochs have funded many sources of environmental skepticism, such as the Heritage Foundation, which has argued that "scientific facts gathered in the past 10 years do not support the notion of catastrophic human-made warming." The brothers have given money to more obscure groups, too, such as the Independent Women's Forum, which opposes the presentation of global warming as a scientific fact in American public schools. Until 2008, the group was run by Nancy Pfotenhauer, a former lobbyist for Koch Industries. Mary Beth Jarvis, a vice-president of a Koch subsidiary, is on the group's board.[66]

To an overwhelming extent, powerful wealthy interests control the media that most people rely on for information and thus help direct the political agenda.[67] The 2010 health care "reform" in the United States ended up being largely made to order by the pharmaceutical and health care industry and will be, therefore, very expensive and still not cover everyone. The financial industry was able to use its power and government connections to limit the 2010 financial "reforms," in the midst of the Great Recession, so that they "shriveled to a set of technical fixes for how the Street should conduct its business."[68]

A culture has developed among political leaders based on the precept that what is good for capitalist business is good for the country. Hence political leaders increasingly see themselves as political entrepreneurs—or the counterparts of economic entrepreneurs. They have convinced themselves that the things they do for corporations—granting lucrative contracts, lessening the effects of "onerous" laws and regulations, and passing laws that favor big business—will not only help them get re-elected, but are actually in the public interest. Within the legal system, the interests of capitalists and their businesses are given every benefit of the doubt.

It is no accident that the oil industry, with hordes of money to lobby and corrupt the system in various ways, is the beneficiary of numerous subsidies and tax advantages. A *New York Times* article described the special advantages enjoyed by the oil industry: "An examination of the American tax code indicates that oil production is among the most heavily subsidized businesses, with tax breaks [estimated at four billion dollars a year] available at virtually every stage of the exploration and extraction process."[69] There is no logical reason to provide subsidies for companies to do what they would do anyway.

Not only has the democratic system been corrupted by money, the leading environmental groups have themselves been co-opted by industry funds. As journalist Johann Hari described it:

After decades of slowly creeping corporate corruption, some of the biggest environmental groups have remade themselves in the image of their corporate backers: they are putting profit before planet. They are supporting a system they know will lead to ecocide, because more revenue will run through their accounts, for a while, as the collapse occurs. At [the 2009] Copenhagen [world climate change meetings], their behavior was so shocking that Lumumba Di-Aping, the lead negotiator for the G-77 bloc of the world's rainforest-rich but cash-poor countries, compared them to the CIA at the height of the cold war, sabotaging whole nations.[70]

A problem that is common to most non-profits (or NGOs, non-governmental organizations) is that it is difficult to sustain income large enough to support an organizational structure that requires a large paid staff and significant infrastructure. Some of the funds can be raised from members and foundations. But foundations, after funding some group or area of interest for a certain period of time, frequently change the direction of their funding. Moreover, foundations themselves get their money from big capital and are notoriously oriented toward establishment interests. If such sources of funding fail, however, where are NGOs to turn? The only other sources are the corporations themselves, which means that the NGOs are forced to depend on those very interests that they ostensibly seek to restrain, compromising their very souls.

Given the power exercised by business interests over the economy, state, media, and even theoretically independent non-profit organizations, it is extremely difficult to effect fundamental changes opposed by corporations. It therefore makes it next to impossible to have a rational and ecologically sound energy policy, health care system, agricultural and food system, industrial policy, trade policy, and educational system. Although the capitalist system in a favorable political environment is able to carry out limited reforms in relation to the environment, as in other areas, such reforms are curtailed long before they reach the point of threatening the economic/social system as a whole. As a result, reforms stop short of addressing the root problems, and the environmental crisis continues to worsen.

There is nothing in the nature of the current system, therefore, that will allow it to pull back before it is too late. To do that, other forces, from the bottom of society—thinking and acting in ways that transcend the logic of the system—will be required.

5. Can Capitalism Go Green?

The most obvious way out [of the climate crisis] is a new round of growth—a giant burst of economic activity designed to replace our fossil-fuel system with something else that will let us go on living just as we do now (or better!), but without the carbon. Even, or especially, as our economy has tanked, we've seized on the idea of green growth as the path out of all our troubles.

—BILL McKIBBEN[1]

Some people who recognize the ecological and social problems that capitalism brings still think that capitalism can and should be reformed. According to Benjamin Barber: "The struggle for the soul of capitalism is . . . a struggle between the nation's economic body and its civic soul: a struggle to put capitalism in its proper place, where it serves our nature and needs rather than manipulating and fabricating whims and wants. Saving capitalism means bringing it into harmony with spirit—with prudence, pluralism and those 'things of the public' . . . that define our civic souls. A revolution of the spirit."[2] William Greider has written a book entitled *The Soul of Capitalism: Opening Paths to a Moral Economy*. There are books that tout the potential of "green capitalism" and the *Natural Capitalism* of Paul Hawken, Amory Lovins, and L. Hunter Lovins. *Green to Gold*, a book by Daniel Esty and Andrew Winston—"printed on acid-free paper made from 100% postconsumer recycled pulp with soy ink"—is subtitled *How Smart Companies Use Environmental Strategy to Innovate, Create Value, and Build Competitive Advantage.*[3] So we can get rich, continue growing the economy, increase consumption without end, and save the planet—all at the same time! How good can it get?

There is, however, a big problem with such thinking. A system that has only one goal, the maximization of profits in an endless quest for the accumulation of capital on an ever-expanding scale, and which thus seeks to transform every single thing on earth into a commodity *with a price*, is a system that is soulless; it can never have a soul, never be green. It can never stand still, but is driven to manipulate and fabricate whims and wants in order to grow and sell more . . . forever. Nothing is allowed to stand in its path.

There are a number of important "out of the box" ecological and environmental thinkers and doers who are highly critical of the status quo and identify with the environmental resistance to the system, but who have nevertheless found ingenious ways to reconcile themselves with capitalism. For example, Hawken and the Lovinses argue that capitalism is not really capitalism unless it fully embraces so-called "natural capital," which means that all will be well if capitalism internalizes everything in nature, bringing the external world under its laws, reducing everything in existence to the status of a commodity—with a price. Consequently, these seemingly nonconformist environmental thinkers do not differ much from a more establishment figure like Al Gore, with his aspirations for a "sustainable capitalism."[4]

Hawken and the Lovinses and many others in the broad tradition they represent—people seeking progressive solutions but finding it impossible to get out of the capitalist framework—are no doubt genuinely good and well-meaning people who are sincerely concerned with the health of the planet. Most are also concerned with issues of social justice. Some truly admirable figures like Wes Jackson and Wendell Berry are working toward concrete low-tech solutions, emphasizing local sustainability and community, while understanding that there is no real silver bullet cure for what ails the planet. We ourselves have been inspired at times by the ideas of such out-of-the- box thinkers.

But there is one box from which it is impossible to escape without confronting it directly: the capitalist economic system. Many, if not most, influential environmental thinkers in the world's rich countries still shy away from such a direct confrontation. Even the increasing numbers of green thinkers who criticize capitalism and its market failures, frequently settle in the end for what they regard as practical solutions directed at creating a tightly controlled humane, green, and non-corporate capitalism, instead of actually getting outside the box of capitalism. Some call for reinventing "the purpose and design of business," or using tax policy to better direct investment and consumption to green ends, or for trade policies that might promote the goods of more sustainable economies.[5] Others suggest eliminating the myriad government subsidies to businesses and taking into account social and ecological consequences of production ("externalities") so as to give rise to "honest prices" that reflect the real costs, including those to the environment.[6] The contradictions and complexities of actually implementing a new way to price commodities, in a system in which the profit is the only god, and power rests in the hands of people who have no interest in doing this, makes all of this an insurmountable task. As David Harvey has said: "If capitalism is forced to internalize" all of the social and environmental costs it generates "it will go out of business. This is the simple truth."[7]

The Mystique of the Market

The remedies proposed by environmental reformers often include maintaining a strong role for private ownership of businesses as well as the role of markets. In many people's minds markets (especially so-called free markets) are an important positive aspect of capitalism because they provide cues telling businesspeople what to invest in, and whether more or less of some product or service should be produced. Markets are also, in this view, the only efficient way of distributing goods. Thus markets are supposed to make sure that what's needed gets produced and what people don't need or want doesn't get produced.

Such claims with regard to market efficiency are frequently based on mystical notions of what markets are—and what the market system is. Indeed, much of this has its basis in a form of circular reasoning: market prices are described as efficient, while efficiency itself is whatever arises from a system of market prices. Widespread market inefficiencies and market failures are downplayed as peripheral issues no matter how pervasive. Negative effects, resulting from the externalization of costs on people and the environment, are often ignored even if they threaten the existence of most human beings and the planet itself.[8] The fact that markets in a capitalist society serve the narrow interest of the accumulation of capital and reinforce power of the wealthy is frequently hidden, since the power relations that lie behind most real markets are not transparent. Often we are told that markets should be self-regulating, and hence "free," which means governments should not intervene. Yet, markets in the real world are dominated by giant corporations, which intervene in numerous ways in their functioning, employing enormous monopoly power. Indeed, economists commonly speak of the *market power* of such giant corporations, in order to refer to their *monopoly power over the market*.

Most discussions of markets ignore not only corporate power but also class power and other forms of social and economic inequality. Market economies are mystifying in that they disguise these vastly unequal relations, generating results that appear accidental—the violence of things rather than the violence of property.[9] The "highest and best use" of a resource or a commodity in a market system is not what benefits the population as a whole, but what benefits those with the greatest purchasing power.

The neoliberal idea of the smoothly operating and efficient self-regulating market society—nothing more than a self-serving myth—dominates much of current policy, and is used to beat down any barriers to economic interests.[10] Rather than a self-regulating market, what we increasingly have today is a society in which private interests increasingly *regulate the state*. For example, in the financial crisis of 2007–2009 the first priority of all of the mature capitalist states was to bail out big capital and big finance, to the tune of trillions of dollars. The population was simply told that the market demanded it, since certain firms were "too big to fail." At the same time that the riches of the wealthiest members of society were being preserved millions of people lost their homes and jobs and slipped into poverty.

The whole notion of the market has become so abstract, and so removed from reality in every way, as economist James K. Galbraith has stated, that "when you come down to it, the word market is a *negation*. It is a word to be applied to the context of any transaction so long as that transaction is not directly dictated by the state."[11]

The Neoliberal Concept of Democracy

The commonplace notion of the opposition between state and market, between public and private, is important. The state represents the realm of political action, in which democracy—the rule of the people, by the people, and for the people—is theoretically possible. In contrast, the market under capitalism represents the rule of capital, by capital, and for capital.

Today, rather than a true democracy we have a plutocracy (rule by moneyed interests) in which some of the formal elements of democracy nonetheless remain. Needless to say a real democracy, as this was classically understood in egalitarian terms, is impossible where income, wealth, and power are concentrated and where inequality is growing, that is, in the normal way of things under capitalism. Hence, ever since the publication in 1942 of Joseph Schumpeter's *Capitalism, Socialism, and Democracy*, in which the neoliberal concept of democracy as a market relationship was first introduced, attempts have been made by defenders of the system to redefine "democracy" in economic terms, transforming it into something nearly opposite its original meaning. In ancient Greece democracy was associated with the rule of the *demos*, i.e., the common people. In contrast, democracy has now been redefined in the United States and some other countries as a system in which individuals simply vote periodically for political entrepreneurs, who seek out their votes much like commercial interests seek out dollars in the marketplace.[12] The essential content of democracy has therefore been eviscerated. So politically corrupted is the U.S. political system that instead of one person, one vote being the rule, an individual's political influence is weighted according to his/her wealth, which determines how responsive politicians are to that individual's interests. Big money, as is well known, provides access to politicians and opens doors. At the same time, corporations themselves "vote" with their dollars, feeding the financial campaign chests of politicians and hiring a phalanx of lobbyists to forward their interests. Politicians frequently end up paying their financial donors back "with interest" for what they receive. As in any business transaction, corporations provide political campaign financing and naturally expect "value added" in return.[13]

The Inversion of the Real

The capitalist system, since it worships what Rachel Carson called "the gods of profit and production" rather than real needs, is unable to supply all people with the essential requirements of a decent life, or, in some cases, life itself.[14] This derives from the fact that capitalism is inherently an alienated system, in which those on the receiving end of the system measure themselves by their distance not only from the rest of the world's population but also from nature itself, glorying in the "conquest of nature." It is a world turned upside down: one that places abstract value above human beings, making it, and not the living, creative forces of nature and humanity, the measure of what is material and productive.

It follows that the various ways of "reforming" capitalism that are promoted by often well-meaning, practical people, who are trying to change things within the parameters of what is allowed by the system, are little more than intellectual contortions: people trying to get around or smooth over basic features of the system because in their eyes a real alternative is unthinkable. In what Derrick Jensen and Aric McBay call the "inversion of what is real," capitalism is seen as more real than the environment; and hence it is capitalism that needs to be saved in the context of the environmental crisis, as opposed to the earth's environment itself.[15]

Not surprisingly, then, the dominant strategies with respect to global warming to be found in environmental circles are concerned not with preserving the planet but with preserving capitalism, the very system that is destroying the earth as we know it. In a speech calling for "urgent action to fight global warming," UN Secretary General Ban Ki-moon said: "We must be actively engaged in confronting the global challenge of climate change, which is a serious threat to development everywhere."[16] In this view, it is not capitalist development, that, by promoting global warming, constitutes a threat to the earth's environment and its inhabitants, but rather global warming that constitutes a threat to capitalist development. What nearly all mainstream solutions to the global environmental problem have in common, as Jensen and McBay write, is that

> they all take industrial capitalism as a given, as that which *must* be saved, as that which must be maintained at all costs (including the murder of the planet, the murder of all that is real), as the independent variable, as primary; and they take the real, physical world—filled with real physical beings who live, die, make the world more diverse—as secondary, as a dependent variable, as something (never someone, of course) that (never who) must conform to industrial capitalism or die. . . . Within this culture, the *world* is consistently less important than *industrial capitalism, the end of the world* is less to be feared than the *end of industrial capitalism.*[17]

The "out of the box" environmental thinkers, who often parade as the most radical and critical green thinkers, but who all too often fall prey to the mystique of capital, are thus unable even to envision, let alone promote, an economic system that has fundamentally different goals and decision-making processes than those that are currently dominant. As cultural theorist Fredric Jameson has said, for many people in this society, "it is easier to imagine the end of the world than to imagine the end of capitalism."[18]

The Morality of "Green Capitalism"

Today green is good. "Being green" has become very fashionable as well as profitable, and corporations are outdoing each other to portray themselves as green and socially responsible. After all, who doesn't want to be considered sustainable? You can buy and wear your Gucci clothes with a clean conscience because the company is helping to protect rain forests by using less paper.[19] *Newsweek* claimed that corporate giants such as Hewlett-Packard, Dell, Johnson & Johnson, Intel, and IBM were the top five green companies of 2009. This was because of their use of renewable sources of energy, their reporting of greenhouse gas emissions (or their lowering of them), and their implementation of formal environmental policies.[20] Some environmentalists and business leaders say that you should "vote with your wallet," by purchasing green products. Environmental problems can be and in some cases are being ameliorated by better production practices (for example, growing organic food or using renewable inputs instead of nonrenewable ones). The business offensive along these lines just prior to the Copenhagen Climate Change meeting was described by the *Guardian* (UK): "Climate change catastrophe can be averted by 'greening' consumer behaviour rather than by curbing economic growth and mass consumerism, leaders of some of the world's biggest businesses including Tesco, Coca-Cola and Reckitt Benckiser argued today."[21]

The mainstream emphasis on corporate responsibility as the solution to the environmental problem can be examined by looking at the case of BP. On April 22, 1999, Sir John Browne, CEO of BP, received an award for Individual Environmental Leadership from the UN Environmental Programme for his leadership in promoting environmental causes. Under Browne's leadership BP had adopted the slogan "Beyond Petroleum," and had acknowledged that greenhouse gases might cause global warming. In 2000 Browne was also awarded *FIRST Magazine's* FIRST Award for Responsible Capitalism for his advances in social responsibility. Browne and BP became symbols of a new green corporate world. "Can business be about more than profits? We think it can"—went a Browne-inspired BP ad. Browne promised growth with environmental cleanliness. Browne was a leading advocate of the "precautionary principle," in which business would refrain from economic activities that might be environmentally destructive.[22]

However, despite BP's "Beyond Petroleum" slogan the company continued its aggressive expansion of oil drilling, even in environmentally sensitive and hazardous areas, such as the Arctic Circle and the deep ocean. Browne argued that there was no conflict between green values and cars that emphasized performance over fuel efficiency. Nor, he insisted, was BP's opposition to government regulation with regard to the environment a contradiction, since socially responsible corporations would police themselves.[23] Under Browne's leadership BP entered an era of extreme cost cutting with regard to safety, which generated greater profits but also greater environmental hazards.

In March 2005 fifteen workers were killed and another 180 injured in chemical fires and explosions at BP's plant in Texas City—later shown to be the fault of drastic cuts in safety personnel.[24] Although Browne resigned as CEO of BP in 2007, BP's practice of putting profits before safety and the environment continued, leading to the Deepwater Horizon oil spill in 2010, after an explosion that killed eleven workers. Oil flowed for three months into the Gulf of Mexico, in the biggest accidental marine oil spill in the history of the oil industry. The spill itself was the result of numerous, egregious reductions in safety standards by BP, associated with a business culture of cost cutting to improve its bottom line.[25]

The fact that BP's celebrated status as a leading "green" company was shown to be mere corporate "greenwashing" should of course hardly surprise us. When noted conservative economist Milton Friedman was asked in 2004 whether John Browne as CEO could go so far with his supposed green convictions as to sacrifice BP's economic interests, Friedman flatly answered: "No. . . . He can do it with his own money. [But] if he pursues those environmental interests in such a way as to run the corporation less effectively for its stockholders, then I think he's being immoral. He's an employee of the stockholders, however elevated his position may appear to be. As such, he has a very strong moral responsibility to them."[26] In other words, it is the fiduciary responsibility of any CEO to pursue the highest profits or the maximum increase in stockholders' equity. If a CEO were so deluded as to think that other values could in some way intrude upon this objective, such that profits would be diminished—say by an oil company cutting back on its drilling or by putting safety and the environment first—then that CEO would soon be out of a job. Quite clearly, John Browne knew the corporate bottom line in this respect, and never let his talk about environmental values and corporate social responsibility interfere with BP's real, exploitative relation to the environment.

The corporate green movement has also reached into consumption, leading to endless hype on "green consumers" and "green markets." All the emphasis in media stories and advertising on sustainable consumption has created would-be green consumers, who feel that by purchasing "sustainable" commodities they can pursue their same consumerist lifestyles and feel virtuous at the same time. However, many so-called green products have been shown to be no better for the environment than their non-green counterparts.[27] As environmentalist Heather Rogers informs us:

> What I learned [while doing research for *Green Gone Wrong*] is that the outcome of industrial organic [food], commodity biofuels, and CO_2 offsetting isn't authentic protection and stewardship of the environment. What's transpiring is a tailoring of environmental crises so they can be dealt with in ways today's economic and political structures deem least threatening to the status quo.[28]

The Corporate Social Responsibility (CSR) programs, although supported by some genuinely concerned individuals, have mainly become marketing opportunities, and somewhat successful as such:

> Companies use CSR programs to build brand loyalty and make personal connections with customers. There can be a payoff: 70 percent of consumers say they would pay a premium for goods from socially responsible companies, according to a recent poll of 1,001 adults.... Of that group, 28 percent said they would pay at least $10 more for a product because of the social responsibility link.[29]

An expert consultant on issues such as "social responsibility" has some doubts about it: "There's often more spin than substance when it comes to social responsibility.... Companies want to take credit for things that they ought to be doing anyway."[30] One of the companies leading the movement, as we have seen, has been BP, one of the least socially responsible companies on Earth. But BP's obfuscating propaganda was effective as indicated by its stock being held in the portfolios of a number of "socially responsible" mutual funds.[31]

Today, mainstream environmentalists, oddly enough, look to Wal-Mart as the leader in corporate responsibility and green business. Thus Wal-Mart, the world's largest corporation in 2009, is celebrated in the Worldwatch Institute's *State of the World, 2010* report as the firm that best exemplifies the move from an exclusive focus on profits to a sustainable business model as its "primary fiduciary responsibility." Former Wal-Mart CEO (now board chairman) Lee Scott is quoted as committing the company in 2005 to "100 percent renewable energy, to create zero waste" (while at the same time admitting he had no idea how Wal-Mart can achieve such goals). We are told that Wal-Mart is now on a "sustainable journey" (at little cost to itself), promoting green values among all of its 1.4 million U.S. employees, who are encouraged to be more sustainable consumers, recycling and eating more healthy meals. Among its other measures, Wal-Mart has pledged to market only wild-caught fish certified by the Marine Stewardship Council (an organization viewed dubiously by Food and Water Watch and by many environmentalists). Its chief concrete environmental commitment, made in 2005, was to become 20 percent more energy efficient by 2013 through cutting the carbon emissions associated with its current stores by 2.5 million metric tons. But by 2006 Wal-Mart's carbon emissions had already risen, by its own admission, another 9 percent. The new stores that were being added in 2007 alone were expected to consume enough electricity to add one million metric tons to its overall greenhouse emissions, exceeding any efficiency gains. As Wes Jackson put it, "When the Wal-Marts of the world say they're going to put in different lightbulbs and get their trucks to get by on half the fuel, what are they going to do with the savings? They're going to open up another box store somewhere. It's just nuts." In the end, Wal-Mart is an economic juggernaut— anything but representative of a new, sustainable economic order.[32] It is known especially for its harsh policies toward labor and its readiness to go to virtually any length (including closing down stores) to prevent the unionization of its workers.

The reality is that none of the proposals for reforming capitalism deal with the essential issue, the bottom line of net gain or profit. For the sake of the environment and our future as a species, the economy cannot keep growing forever with more and more goods and services (green or not) consumed per person. But if the economy doesn't grow, how are jobs going to be created and maintained? Experience has shown that slow or no growth in a capitalist economy is a disaster for working people.

Is Reversing Global Climate Change Compatible with Capitalism?

Let's put aside corporate greenwashing efforts, the systemic imperative to growth and environmental exploitation, and the question of the role of technology under capitalism and take a look at some of the proposed technical ways to deal with global climate change—currently the most critical problem facing the earth and its inhabitants—without disturbing capitalism.

TECHNOLOGIES THAT ARE MORE ENERGY EFFICIENT, LESS HARMFUL, AND/OR USE FEWER MATERIAL INPUTS

Some proposals to enhance energy efficiency—such as helping people tighten up and insulate their old homes so that less fuel is required for winter heating, and the use of simple rooftop solar water heaters—are just plain common sense. Machinery, including household appliances and automobiles, is continually becoming more energy efficient—a normal part of the system, sometimes coaxed by government regulations. Nevertheless, it is important to note that increased energy efficiency usually leads to lower costs of use, but also increased use, and often increased size as well, as in automobiles and refrigerators—so that the amount of energy used is frequently increased, or the energy savings are less than they would be if product size remained the same. People may drive their fuel-efficient Toyota Prius more miles and leave on the efficient LED lighting more hours than with more energy-consuming technologies. They may think that they are doing the earth a favor by buying hybrid SUVs that are more fuel-efficient than non-hybrids, but still use a lot more fuel than a smaller vehicle.

There are proposals to provide less polluting technologies, particularly solar, wind, and water power. It is certainly true that this is the way to go in generating energy, as opposed to fossil fuels, agrofuels, or nuclear energy. There is also the possibility of combining hydropower with either wind or solar power by pumping water uphill during the day when energy from wind and solar are available and then allowing the water to return through turbines, generating electricity at night if needed. But these sources of energy do not provide a free lunch with respect to the environment, and hence do not allow for unlimited economic expansion without cost. They frequently come with their own problems. There is renewed interest in hydropower, especially in smaller-scale projects—although large-scale projects continue to be developed in Asia and South America. The damage to the environment and to humans caused by large dams—forests inundated, species destroyed, seawater intrusion and the killing off of mangroves in deltas, and relocation of indigenous peoples—has generated a movement to try to stop such projects.

The earth's geothermal energy can be safely developed in some areas (Iceland has done quite a bit with this source of energy) and holds promise, although appropriate locations are difficult to find and drilling for such projects in northern California and Switzerland triggered earthquakes.[33] Resource extraction needed for some of the "clean" technologies, such as the rare earths required for wind electric generators and hybrid car batteries, come with their own environmental issues.[34]

While some of the proposals make sense, the misguided push to "green" agrofuels (biofuels made from agricultural crops such as corn, soybeans, rapeseed, and palm oil) has been enormously detrimental to the environment and people. The idea is to replace oil-derived gasoline and diesel by producing the liquid fuels ethanol and biodiesel from farmed crops. Not only has the growth of the agrofuel industry put food and auto fuel in direct competition, pushing food prices higher, but the production of agrofuels also sometimes actually uses more energy to grow and transport and process the crop than the energy obtained. In addition, significant air and water pollution is frequently associated with the growing and processing of crops for liquid fuels.[35]

Tropical forests are being cut down to plant oil palms, to supply oil to produce biodiesel (in addition to its customary use as a cooking oil and in cosmetics), resulting in displacement of indigenous peoples and massive emissions of CO_2 as trees are burned and soils disturbed. Conversion of forests to produce oil palm to make "green" biodiesel ends up increasing CO_2 emissions, even in the fairly long term. It is estimated that it will take four hundred years of diesel production of palm oil from these plantations to "pay back" the environment for the CO_2 emissions occurring during preparation and planting of oil palm trees.

Another idea for producing "green" liquid fuels is to convert plant cellulose to alcohol, although it is not yet economically feasible to do so. One of the potential materials, the crop "waste," considered to be one of the important feedstocks for this endeavor, is not waste at all. The return to the soil of crop residues is essential for maintaining organic matter, which has such positive effects on crop yields. Another avenue being explored is the use of algae that make oil. However, this has its own potential problems such as the amount of land needed and the possibility that genetically modified algae will be used, with unknown consequences if they escape into the environment.

Instead of rethinking the entire system as environmental problems develop, people look for silver bullets—technologies such as agrofuels that will "solve" the problem. However, it is not uncommon to discover later that the silver bullet itself causes other problems. For example, in order to find a replacement for ozone-depleting chemicals used in refrigerators and air conditioners as well as insulating foam, HFCs (hydrofluorocarbons) were introduced as a substitute in the 1990s.[36] Though this did help the protective ozone layer recover, HFCs turn out to have over 4,000 times the heat-trapping ability of CO_2, thus worsening global warming. The increase in atmospheric HFCs from leakage from junked refrigerators and air conditioners is projected to be large enough by 2050 to account for six years' worth of CO_2 emissions.

There are technologies that allow for some kind of conservation, lessening the throughput of resources and energy, generating less waste, reducing toxins, etc. But increased efficiency in the use of energy and resources tends, as we have seen, to result in the expansion of the capitalist economic system as a whole, negating any reductions in energy and resource use per unit of output. This is known as the Jevons Paradox, after nineteenth-century economist William Stanley Jevons, who first raised the issue in his book *The Coal Question.* Jevons pointed out that every new steam engine was more efficient in its use of coal than the one before, and yet the introduction of each more efficient engine led to the consumption of greater amounts of coal due to the expansion of production. The Jevons Paradox is now widely recognized by environmentalists as a key reason why technology alone—outside the transformation of social relations—cannot solve the ecological contradictions of capitalism.[37] As philosopher Hannah Arendt put it in *The Human Condition*: "Under modern conditions, not destruction but conservation spells ruin because the very durability of conserved objects is the greatest impediment to the turnover process [of capital], whose constant gain in speed is the only constancy left wherever it has taken hold."[38]

HIGH-TECH/HIGH-RISK SOLUTIONS

The fact that accumulation is the single drumbeat of capitalist society means that ecological systems, and the biological-health systems of species, are stretched to the limits, leading to ever-increasing risk. This has led sociologists to speak of the emergence of a "risk society," as a product of capitalism and modernity.[39] Toxic chemicals, radiation, and other hazards pervade our environment and our bodies, with no attempt to discern the full effects—or even to test most of the chemicals, despite their frequent carcinogenic, teratogenic, and mutagenic effects. It is enough for the system that such technologies are useful in expanding the economy at low cost to business. The consequences are dealt with in terms of so-called risk management, attempting to discern (while underestimating and playing down) the number of deaths per million that constitute "acceptable risk."[40] In a society organized in this way it is natural enough to respond to the threat to the planet represented by global warming by turning to riskier and riskier technologies, continually upping the general level of risk. Where "progress" is confused with higher profit margins, which often means the willingness to take on greater risk, such a solution may even seem rational.

The risk-society issue is immediately evident when the question of nuclear power as a solution to global warming arises. Some scientists concerned with climate change, including James Lovelock and James Hansen, see nuclear power as an energy alternative and as a partial technological answer to the use of fossil fuels—one that is much preferable to the growing use of coal. However, nuclear energy at present releases 9 to 25 times the carbon emissions of wind energy, due to uranium refining, transport, and reactor construction. Although the technology of nuclear energy has improved somewhat with third-generation nuclear plants, and although there is now the possibility (still not a reality) of fourth-generation nuclear energy, the dangers of nuclear power are still enormous—given radioactive waste lasting hundreds and thousands of years, the social management of complex systems, and the sheer level of risk involved. The 2011 post earthquake/tsunami disaster at Japan's Fukushima Dai-Ichi facility once again illustrates the ongoing dangers and immense risks associated with dependence on nuclear power.

The breeder nuclear reactor—a third-generation nuclear technology currently available and often presented as an alternative—has similar problems to those of conventional fission reactors, though producing less low-level radioactive waste and able to reuse the spent fuel, thereby alleviating the problem of limited uranium reserves. However, they also generate nuclear materials closer to weapons grade that can be more readily reprocessed for nuclear weapons. This close connection between nuclear power and nuclear weapons development is of course a major concern for all humanity.

Nuclear plants take about ten years to build and are extremely costly and uneconomic. It has been estimated that to satisfy the world's electrical power demands through nuclear energy it would require building a nuclear power plant every day for the next forty-three years. If a mere 5 percent of these were built it would double the world's current nuclear power installations worldwide. The result would be an increased likelihood of what sociologist Charles Perrow has called "normal accidents," as these extremely high-risk facilities proliferate. There are all sorts of reasons, therefore, to be extremely wary of nuclear power as any kind of environmental solution. To go in that direction would clearly be a Faustian bargain.[41]

A number of vast geoengineering schemes have been proposed either to take CO_2 out of the atmosphere or to increase the reflectance of sunlight back into space, away from Earth. These include:

- Finding ways of absorbing carbon more effectively, such as fertilizing the oceans with iron to stimulate algal growth to absorb carbon, and reforesting the planet with genetically altered fast-growing trees.

- Various proposals to decrease solar energy absorbed by the Earth by means of enhanced sunlight reflection schemes, such as deploying huge white islands in the oceans to restore the albedo effect; creating large satellites to reflect incoming sunlight; contaminating the stratosphere with sulfur dioxide particles that reflect light and promote global dimming.

- Geoengineering carbon sequestration on a massive scale. Here the assumption is that physics and economics will allow the capture of carbon, and the use of large machines distributed around the world will make it possible to scrub CO_2 from the atmosphere itself instead of from individual industrial plant emissions. After trapping CO_2 on an adsorbing material, it would then be liquefied for disposal.[42]

No one knows what detrimental side effects might occur from such huge schemes—attempts to play God with the planet. The sheer complexity of the problems raised suggests the enormous, planetary-risk nature of such ventures. For example, stimulating algal growth by applying iron to oceans might just lead to more "dead zones" when the algae die and fall to the lower depths, harming other aquatic life. Dumping sulfur dioxide into the stratosphere to block sunlight could reduce photosynthesis throughout the planet.

"CLEAN COAL"

One common technological solution proposed is the shift to what is referred to as "clean coal" as a way of expanding the production of fossil fuels—but without carbon emissions. The U.S. government has poured billions of dollars into supporting such clean coal research. Although clean coal is not a reality (and never can be), the mere idea is used to defend continued coal production and the building of more dirty coal plants. The clean-coal technology claim is based on what is called carbon capture and storage (CCS) technology. This technology is designed to remove carbon from the air prior to its being released into the atmosphere and turn it into a non-harmful substance that can be injected into geological formations or into the ocean. Even the most optimistic scenarios, however, do not see CCS technology as available until 2030—way too late to deal with the immediate climate change problem. The technology, while nascent, has never been used on an industrial scale. Moreover, it carries with it enormous economic costs—with price increases from the implementation of CCS technology estimated to be in the range of 21 to 91 percent. The fuel needs of plants employing CCS technology are expected to go up by 25 percent. A May 2011 report by the American Physical Society on the physics of DAC (direct air capture) of carbon dioxide concluded:

> With optimistic assumptions about some important technical parameters, the cost of this system is estimated to be of the order of $600 or more per metric ton of CO_2. Significant uncertainties in the process parameters result in a wide, asymmetric range associated with this estimate, with higher values being more likely than lower ones. Thus, DAC is not currently an economically viable approach to mitigating climate change . . . Since a 1000-megawatt coal power plant emits about six million metric tons of CO_2 per year, a DAC system consisting of structures 10 meters high that removes CO_2 from the atmosphere as fast as this coal plant emits CO_2 would require structures whose total length would be about 30 kilometers. Large quantities of construction materials and chemicals would be required. It is likely that the full cost of the benchmark DAC system scaled to capture six million metric tons of CO_2 per year would be much higher than alternative strategies providing equivalent decarbonized electricity.[43]

The injection of captured carbon into the ocean could increase the acidity of the ocean with consequences potentially as large as climate change itself. The ramifications of attempting to store the captured carbon dioxide in geological formations is still uncertain, though it is clear that the escape of large amounts of the gas could be dangerous (residents near an African lake were suffocated in 1986 when a natural pocket of carbon dioxide escaped). For all of these reasons, clean coal is largely a hoax. The real priority, as James Hansen indicates, is to stop building new coal plants and to retire those that exist. If the coal reserves are burned climate change will become unstoppable and catastrophic. CCS technology also does not address the many other environmental damages caused by coal production and coal plants: mountaintop removal, long-wall mining, plus all the mercury, arsenic, sulfates, and other air and water pollutants that come with the coal system.[44]

LOW-TECH SOLUTIONS

Also proposed are a number of low-tech ways to sequester carbon such as increasing reforestation and using ecological soil management to increase soil organic matter (which is composed mainly of carbon). Most of the management techniques for increasing soil organic matter—use of cover crops, return of crop residue to the soil, integrating livestock and crop farming once again, and using better crop rotations—should be done for their own sake because organic material helps to improve soils in many ways. As agricultural soil organic matter content increases and forests grow (and the soil underneath the forest also increases in organic matter), this keeps at least some CO_2 out of the atmosphere. Thus reforestation, by pulling carbon from the atmosphere, is sometimes thought of as constituting negative emissions.

Another scheme for increasing stored carbon in the soil is to incorporate "biochar," the product of relatively low temperature burning with limited oxygen. This char is very stable and is believed to be one of the factors responsible for the maintenance of soil fertility in long abandoned fields in the Amazon basin (these dark soils are referred to as *terra preta de indio*). However, forests must be cut down to produce large quantities of biochar, and croplands will have to be used to grow residue to burn—and about half of the carbon contained in these materials will end up in the atmosphere during the combustion process.

Some low-tech solutions may help, but obviously cannot solve the problem given an expanding economic system, especially since trees planted now take a long time to sequester meaningful amounts of carbon, can be cut down later, and carbon stored as soil organic matter may later be converted to CO_2 if practices are changed. However, if practiced, widely increasing soil organic matter might provide a temporary slowing down of the rate of increase of atmospheric CO_2.

Cap-and-Trade and Other Market Schemes

Government regulation of polluting industries has worked to some extent and can in the future if the regulations address the actual problems and the regulators are not in bed with those being regulated, which, however, is the normal case in the present system. A struggle for increased government regulation with respect to the environment, particularly if structured to respond to the needs of the actual population as a result of constant public pressure, is a necessary immediate response to the environmental problem.

But many environmentalists, unable to imagine a non-capitalist economy, and responding to what they consider practical— that is, what the reigning economic interests are willing to accept—have endorsed market-based "solutions" to environmental problems. These run the gamut from paying businesses to be more ecologically sound (such as "green payments" for farmers to use practices that reduce soil erosion), to the heavy taxation of fossil fuel use, to giving or selling tradable rights to pollute after imposing a cap on emissions of the pollutant.

Until the last couple of years, the darling of market-oriented solutions to carbon emissions was "cap-and-trade." This involves placing a cap on the allowable level of greenhouse gas emissions and then distributing, either by fee or by auction, permits that allow industries to emit carbon dioxide and other greenhouse gases. Those corporations that have more permits than they need may sell them to other firms that want additional permits to pollute. Such schemes invariably include "offsets" that act like medieval indulgences, allowing corporations to continue to pollute as long as they buy good grace through helping to curtail pollution somewhere else, perhaps in the third world.

How did cap-and-trade, as opposed to taxing pollution or simply legally mandating reductions in emissions, go from a theory to a near consensus? According to a 2009 article in the *New York Times*:

> The answer is not to be found in the study of economics or environmental science, but in the realm where most policy debates are ultimately settled: politics. Many members of Congress remember the painful political lesson of 1993, when President Bill Clinton proposed a tax on all forms of energy, a plan that went down to defeat and helped take the Democratic majority in Congress down with it a year later. *Cap and trade, by contrast, is almost perfectly designed for the buying and selling of political support through the granting of valuable emissions permits to favor specific industries and even specific Congressional districts.*[45]

Cap-and-trade—originally proposed by conservatives for reducing sulfur dioxide (a significant contributor to acid rain) emissions from power plants—has gone out of favor in the United States as a response to carbon emissions because conservatives now claim it is a new tax, and some of the political liberals in Congress are aware of its failure in Europe. It is clear that this proposed solution is much less efficient than a straight tax or mandate for lowering pollution, partly because it tends to put a floor under existing emissions, partly because it promotes offsets that "reduce" emissions only on paper, not in reality.

In theory, carbon cap-and-trade would stimulate technological innovation to increase energy and commodity output per amount of carbon dioxide emitted. In practice, however, it has not led to carbon dioxide emission reductions in areas where it has been introduced, such as Europe. The main result of carbon trading has been enormous profits for some corporations and individuals and the creation of a subprime carbon market.[46]

Carbon offsets are invariably part of cap-and-trade schemes but also can be stand-alone projects. You can now travel wherever you want, guilt-free, by purchasing carbon "offsets," such as having a few trees planted somewhere, and thus supposedly cancel out the environmental effects of your trip. The lack of verification and long-term commitment of these supposed offsets can result in fraudulent or poorly designed and carried out projects that will not be enough to compensate truly for the CO_2 emitted and supposedly offset.[47] In addition, there are no prohibitions against changing conditions sometime in the future that will result in carbon dioxide release to the atmosphere.

Europe dominates the $144 billion a year (in 2009) greenhouse gas market. A primary offset purchased by many European companies has been for Chinese firms to destroy HFC-23, a by-product of producing the gas HFC-22, used as a refrigerant. One molecule of HFC-23 in the atmosphere has about ten thousand times the heat retention of one molecule of CO_2. It turns out that companies can make a lot of money destroying HFC-23. There is evidence that some plants in China have been producing more refrigerant than they can sell in order to have more HFC-23 that they can be paid to destroy.[48] About half of all offsets approved by the United Nations through the summer of 2010 are for credits for HFC-23 destruction. As Clare Perry of the Environmental Investigation Agency has stated, "It would be far cheaper and more effective to directly finance the factories to deal with the HFC-23 problem rather than use this kind of byzantine financing."[49]

For James Hansen cap-and-trade is the "temple of doom" and "worse than nothing" because it prevents effective action directly limiting carbon through regulations and a properly designed tax, while giving people the impression that something is being done.[50] Indeed, the various technofixes discussed above associated with today's green technology and markets—more efficient and/or cleaner energy production and use, better regulations, cap-and-trade of greenhouse gases, carbon offsets, etc.—are all roads to climate catastrophe rather than climate protection. "Green capitalism," even if products are produced using the utmost environmental care and designed for easy reuse, offers no way out of a system that must expand exponentially and thus, continue to ratchet up its use of natural resources, its chemical pollution, its contaminated sewage sludge, its garbage, and its many other toxic substances. Some of these "fixes" will probably slow down the rate of environmental destruction, but the magnitude of the needed changes dwarfs these approaches.

Indeed, the problem with all of these approaches is that they allow the economy to continue on the same disastrous course it is currently following. The economy can keep on growing and we can go on consuming all we want (or as much as our income and wealth allow)—driving greater distances in our more fuel-efficient cars, living in very large but well-insulated homes, consuming all sorts of new products made by green corporations, and so on. All we need to do is support the new green technologies and be "good" about separating out waste that can be composted or reused in some form, and we can go on living pretty much as before, in an economy of perpetual growth and profits.

The Need for Sustainable Human Development

The seriousness of the climate change problem arising from human-generated carbon dioxide and other greenhouse gas emissions has led to notions that it is merely necessary to reduce carbon footprints (a difficult problem in itself). The reality is that there are numerous, interrelated, and growing ecological problems arising from a system geared to the infinitely expanding accumulation of capital. What needs to be reduced is not just *carbon footprints* but *ecological footprints*, which means that economic expansion on the world level and especially in the rich countries needs to be reduced, even cease. At the same time, many poor countries need to expand their economies, requiring an even bigger cut in the ecological footprints of rich economies to make room for development in the periphery.

The new principles we should promote under these circumstances are those of sustainable human development. This means *enough* for everyone and no more. Human development would certainly not be hindered, and could even be considerably enhanced, for the benefit of all by an emphasis on sustainable human, rather than unsustainable economic, development.[51]

A drastic transformation in global energy use—staying within the solar energy budget—will be required to overcome the problem of climate change. To give some idea of the incredible effort needed to keep global warming to *only* 2 degrees C (3.6 degrees F) simply by technical means, about 80 percent of all of the energy used in the world (13 out of 16 trillion watts) would need to be replaced by CO_2-neutral technologies. According to a *New Yorker* article profiling inventor Saul Griffith, accomplishing this "would require building the equivalent of all the following: a hundred square metres of new solar cells, fifty square metres of new solar-thermal reflectors, and one Olympic swimming pool's volume of genetically engineered algae (for biofuels) every second for the next twenty-five years; one three-hundred-foot-diameter wind turbine every five minutes; one hundred-megawatt geothermal-powered steam turbine every eight hours; and one three-gigawatt nuclear power plant every week."[52] All of this new construction would of course mean a huge, if temporary, increase in energy demands. Griffith has explained: "Everyone sees climate change as a problem in the domain of scientists and engineers. . . . But it's not enough to say that we need some nerds to invent a new energy source and some other nerds to figure out a carbon-sequestration technology—and you should be skeptical about either of those things actually happening. There are a lot of ideas out there, but nothing nearly as radical as the green-tech hype. We've been working on energy, as a society, for a few thousand years, and especially for the last two hundred years, so we've already turned over most of the stones."[53] Regardless of whether major advances in cleaner energy production are coming soon, the magnitude of the climate change problem calls for drastic reductions in energy use through conservation and alterations in lifestyle. This requires radical transformations in human priorities—not just placing one's hopes in technological fixes.

The reality is that the major environmental problems we face today—of which climate change is only one—cannot be solved by means of technological or market-based solutions while keeping existing social relations intact. Rather, what is needed most is a transformation in social relations: in community, culture, and economy, in how we relate to each other as human beings, and how we relate to the planet. What is needed, in other words, is an ecological revolution.

6. An Ecological Revolution Is Not Just Possible—It's Essential

> I am convinced there is only one way to eliminate these grave evils, namely through the establishment of a socialist economy. . . . A planned economy which adjusts production to the needs of the community, would distribute the work to be done among all those able to work and would guarantee a livelihood to every man, woman, and child. The education of the individual, in addition to promoting his own innate abilities, would attempt to develop in him a sense of responsibility for his fellow men in place of the glorification of power and success in our present society.
>
> —ALBERT EINSTEIN[1]

The analysis in earlier chapters, if correct, points to the fact that the ecological crisis cannot be solved within the logic of the present economic/political/social system. The various suggestions for doing so have no hope of success. The system of world capitalism is clearly unsustainable in: (1) its quest for never-ending accumulation of capital leading to production that must constantly expand to provide profits; (2) its agriculture and food system that pollutes the environment and still does not allow universal access to a sufficient quantity and quality of food; (3) its rampant destruction of the environment; (4) its continual enhancing of the inequality of income and wealth within and between countries; (5) its search for technological magic bullets as a way of avoiding the growing social and ecological problems arising from the system's own functioning and operations; and (6) its promotion and rewarding of personality characteristics that lead to loss of connection with fellow humans, with communities, and with nature.

What Can Be Done Now?

To call for an ecological revolution against capitalist society is of course to open oneself to the criticism that such a solution would simply take too long to effect even if it were possible, given the sheer urgency of the global ecological crisis, which presents us with tipping points a decade or two (or even less) away. Shouldn't we be thinking about what can be done now? Indeed, the urgency of the situation cries out for immediate action. But any actions to be taken today, if they are to be effective, must be framed in terms of the larger goal of an ecological revolution. As Paul Sweezy wrote in "Capitalism and the Environment" in 1989:

> What has to be done to resolve the environmental crisis, hence also to insure that humanity has a future, is to replace capitalism with a social order based on an economy devoted not to maximizing private profit and accumulating ever more capital but rather to meeting real human needs and restoring the environment to a sustainably healthy condition. This, in a nutshell, is the meaning of revolutionary change today.[2]

But obviously this can't happen all at once. Such an ecological revolution must start from where we currently stand, recognizing that we must try to address the immediate, most pressing dangers, while simultaneously working toward the longer goal of replacing capitalism with a more humane and sustainable social order.

There are things that have been done and that can be done even within capitalist society to lessen the system's negative effects on the environment and people. Much more can be accomplished, however, if we focus on what needs to be done, rather than on the limits the system imposes. We cannot, for example, refuse to do what is absolutely necessary to protect the earth, just because the profit system seemingly will not allow it. We must push the capitalist system to its bottom line in terms of sustainability criteria—and then cross that bottom line: putting people and the environment before profits. History teaches that although capitalism has at times responded to environmental movements—without which the system might have by now completely destroyed the environment—at a certain point, at which the system's underlying accumulation drive is affected, its resistance to environmental demands stiffens. Those with vested interests move quickly to block or disable changes that threaten their profits or the system as a whole, however necessary these are to protect humanity and the earth. "Long before that point [at which the existence of the system itself is threatened] is reached," Sweezy wrote, "the capitalist class, including the state which it controls, mobilizes its defenses to repulse the environmental-protection measures perceived as dangerously extreme."[3]

We must therefore recognize that even if everything that can be done inside capitalism is done, it won't solve the underlying problem—an economic system that causes environmental and social damage in the very way it functions. This means that for meaningful and enduring solutions to our environmental problems, a very strong social-political movement is needed, both to counter the weight of corporate interests and to change the system itself. Some people are making the choice to live more in concert with the environment, and this is a good thing, one to be encouraged. However, mass movements and major restructuring of the economy and society are essential if we are to save the planet. Such mass movements must struggle for measures to save humanity and the planet in the present, while recognizing that this ultimately points to the need for a revolution in our entire way of life in the future.

People as individuals and, more effectively, as part of organizations and mass movements, can demand major changes. Some organizations have come to the conclusion that direct action—for example, blocking trains bringing coal to power plants—is necessary. They may well be right to have concluded that only those actions that disrupt the system at environmentally strategic points have any chance of bringing meaningful change. But even if you are not ready to go to such lengths, there are many areas in which it is important to struggle in the here and now to address urgent environmental problems, and at the same time create the basis in our movements and culture for the even bigger changes that must follow.

This is not an exhaustive list, and is arranged in no particular order, but constitutes what we believe might reasonably be thought of as a short-term agenda for environmental activists, prioritizing those issues that are most important:

- Institute a carbon tax of the kind proposed by James Hansen, in which 100 percent of the dividends go back to the public. This would encourage conservation, while placing the burden on those with the largest carbon footprints and the most wealth. If the tax is returned to the population with the same amount going to each person, poor people and others using less than the average amount of energy will get more back than they paid in increased costs. In contrast, those using a lot more energy than the average person will end up getting much less back than the extra they paid because of the tax.

- Block new coal-fired plants (without sequestration of gaseous carbon dioxide, which is not feasible at present) and close down old ones. Although some will regard this as extreme, it is absolutely necessary in order to protect the planet from climate change.[4]

- Place a block on any attempt to use tar sands and oil/gas shale production to replace diminishing crude oil supplies, since these are even more dangerous from a climate change standpoint, emitting larger amounts of carbon dioxide. Exploiting these sources does other environmental damage as well—to land and ground and surface waters.

- Make the United States participate with the other nations of the world to draft a world agreement for a drastic reduction in carbon emissions. This should follow the *Peoples' Agreement* of the World Peoples' Conference on Climate Change and the Rights of Mother Earth (see Appendix). The 2013 to 2017 period demands at least 50 percent reduction in domestic emissions of the developed countries based on 1990s levels, excluding carbon markets and offset mechanisms. Agreements must be binding on all parties. A fund needs to be provided to help developing countries pay for the costs associated with adapting to climate change.

- Push for the wealthy countries, especially the United States, to back contraction and convergence in carbon emissions at the world level, moving to uniform world per capita emissions, with cutbacks far deeper in the rich countries with large per capita carbon footprints.[5]

- End the extraction of natural resources that are prone to excessive environmental damage. Safer drilling in the deep waters of the Gulf of Mexico is preferable to unsafe practices. And a stronger regulatory agency that oversees this drilling is preferable to one that sees industry's interests as more important than those of the public's interests. But the exploitation of difficult-to-get resources in fragile areas, such as deep-sea oil, should not be allowed at all.

- Make more efficient use of energy, *together* with reducing energy use. More efficient cars do not necessarily lead to less energy use. However, if people are encouraged to use their more energy-efficient cars/lighting/gadgets less, it might help the environment. We should encourage use of the tremendous quantity of waste heat from industry, especially power-generating plants, to heat (and/or cool) homes and offices. Waste heat can also be used to keep greenhouses productive in cold seasons.

- Provide for all of the world's energy needs with wind, water, and sunlight (WWS), eliminating fossil fuel use—without resorting to biofuels or nuclear power. This means relying on wind, wave, geothermal, small hydroelectric, tidal, solar photovoltaic (PV), and concentrated solar power (CSP) systems. Transportation technologies consistent with WWS systems must rely primarily on battery-electric vehicles, hydrogen fuel cells and hybrid hydrogen fuels, and in the case of aircraft, liquefied hydrogen. There needs to be a massive, planned shift of energy systems worldwide to WWS technologies.[6]

- Promote mass transit, including high-speed trains for intercity travel and light rail and dedicated bus lanes in cities, to reduce car dependency. The huge subsidies presently directed at private car use should be shifted to more efficient and environmentally sound forms of public transport.

- Make the U.S. EPA enhance its efforts to ensure that environmental justice concerns are integral to its decision-making process. Poor neighborhoods, villages, and countries should not be used as dumping grounds for toxic garbage, incinerators, or for locating especially polluting industries.

- Encourage a more sustainable agriculture that eliminates wherever possible ecologically destructive industrial agricultural practices. The inhumane raising of farm animals under crowded and unhealthy factory-like conditions, which necessitate routine antibiotic use that promotes new resistant bacteria to develop, must be stopped—for social, humanitarian, and ecological reasons. People in many developed countries have the possibility to purchase food directly from producers at farmers' markets and through community-supported agriculture (CSA) farms.[7]

- Combat the extreme rifts between city and country, in which out-of-control urban development and sprawl eradicate rural areas, and at the same time place more demands on rural areas. Huge city slums must be eliminated. The ownership of vast agricultural estates by a small part of the population in most countries must be transcended through equitable land reform and redistribution, allowing for a more rational agriculture and settlement of people.

- Reverse the privatization of the world's freshwater and make freshwater a *right* of all people, under public control and managed in the public interest. Both water conservation and the cleanup of water resources should be top priorities. The rapid drawing down of groundwater resources must cease.[8]

- Push for binding international agreements that limit fishing by factory-size ships; stop the catch of endangered species such as the bluefin tuna; and drastically reduce the catch of species that are in decline. We should only promote the farming of fish species that can be fed non-fish aquatic diets (many farmed fish are fed other, smaller fish, which depletes the lower parts of the ocean's food chain and endangers wild species) and grown in ways that do not allow diseases or parasites to enter the wild population.

- Protect habitats of threatened and endangered species around the world to ensure the biological diversity in the face of what is now called "the sixth extinction."[9]

- Develop a better social safety-net system, one with universal health care, expanded social security, better protection against unemployment, living wages, and access to an adequate quantity and quality of food.

- Create new jobs for workers displaced from manufacturing plants, through a massive effort to develop and implement greener technologies and industries and to increase reliance on small-scale farming. We need to struggle—in the words of President Franklin D. Roosevelt in his 1944 State of the Union address to Congress, in which he outlined the need for an Economic Bill of Rights—for "the right to a useful and remunerative job . . . the right to earn enough to provide adequate food and clothing and recreation . . . the right of every family to a decent home . . . the right to adequate medical care and the opportunity to achieve and enjoy good health . . . the right to a good education."[10]

- Achieve a more equitable distribution of resources, using every means at our disposal, including taxation, public works, building affordable housing for the poor—whatever will do the job—to create a more equal distribution of resources.

- Stop the "revolving door," through which elements of the power elite rotate between business/lobbying and working for government agencies or being members of Congress.

- Bring an end to the imposition of increased environmental risks on people due to race, class, gender, and nationality. Environmental justice is a key to any genuine environmental movement in the present and future. The environmental movement must be built from the ground up on the basis of environmental justice and sustainability. As Angela Park eloquently argued in her report, *Everybody's Movement: Environmental Justice and Climate Change* (2009), the movement against global warming can only be *everybody's movement* if it places environmental justice issues at the center of its understanding of the necessary change.[11]

- Cut military spending massively across-the-board and all forms of imperial expenditures. Close down foreign military bases. Shift this spending to social needs and the defense of the environment.

- Perhaps the most important thing that people can do—while participating with groups in struggles to improve the environment—is to talk about the larger issue of how the economic system itself promotes environmental destruction and to join with others who have this understanding in working for change.

Emerging Radical Movements

All over the world radical struggles and experiments are occurring in the interstices of capitalist society aimed at creating a more just and sustainable society. If history tells us anything, it is that progressive change occurs in response to people organizing and fighting for it. So something that can be done now is to join organizations committed to the creation of a new society—ones that are willing to work in coalitions with other groups and understand that the broad struggle for a better world has goals of social and economic justice as well as a healthy environment.

Indigenous peoples today, given new impetus by the ongoing revolutionary struggle in Bolivia, are reinforcing a new ethic of responsibility to the earth. La Vía Campesina, a global peasant-farmer organization, is promoting new forms of ecological agriculture, as is Brazil's MST (Movimento dos Trabalhadores Rurais Sem Terra), as well as Cuba and Venezuela. Venezuelan president Hugo Chávez has raised the social and environmental reasons to work to get rid of the oil-rentier economic model—remarkable, given that Venezuela is a major oil exporter.[12] The climate justice movement is demanding egalitarian and anticapitalist solutions to the climate crisis. The World Peoples' Conference on Climate Change and the Rights of Mother Earth, held in April 2010 in Bolivia, drew tens of thousands of people from around the world. One of the principal messages of the conference was that the capitalist economic system was the main culprit in causing harm to the environment.

Everywhere, radical, essentially anticapitalist strategies are emerging, based on other ethics and forms of organization, rather than the profit motive: eco-villages such as Gaviotas in Colombia; the new urban transportation systems pioneered in Curitiba in Brazil and elsewhere; experiments in permaculture; community-supported agriculture (CSA farms, mentioned above, where people purchase shares in the food that the farm produces, thus bypassing commercial outlets); Detroit citizens taking action to provide services and food in urban settings because of the absence of effective government programs; the urban farming efforts begun in Milwaukee by Will Allen to bring fresh food directly into the low-income neighborhoods; farming and industrial cooperatives in Venezuela; and many others.

On May 8, 2011, youth in 25 countries and 5 continents marched in protests over the failure to address climate change, as part of the iMatter campaign initiated by 16-year-old Alec Loorz, who four years earlier, at the age of 12, founded the organization "Kids vs Global Warming." Loorz argues that we need a "revolution" in our relation to the environment, and that if the "ruling generation" won't do it on their own maybe they will act in response to the militant protests of the world's youth. He has filed a lawsuit, along with children in all 50 states of the United States, suing the government for "allowing money to be more powerful than the survival" of the younger generation, and demanding the creation of an "atmospheric trust" to protect the climate for future generations.[13]

The international youth climate justice movement—though its U.S. branch has recently backed off (at the leadership level) from its earlier more radical, anti-capitalist stance—points to the possibility of a massive, militant, youth counterculture developing within the climate movement.[14]

The World Social Forum has given voice to many of these aspirations for the creation of a new, more sustainable world. As Speth has stated: "The international social movement for change—which refers to itself as 'the irresistible rise of global anti-capitalism'—is stronger than many may imagine and will grow stronger."[15]

Long-range Solutions: Planning for a New Society

None of the immediate goals proposed above is feasible, even in the short run, unless the demands are part of a massive movement that is not afraid to do what needs to be done, and refuses to let the bottom line of the profit system determine the future of the earth and humanity. Where any serious attempt to tackle environmental issues is concerned, conflict with the system arises quickly, and the more the question of ecological revolution comes to the fore the more it becomes a question of a revolution against capitalism. This is particularly true where long-range issues, involving democratic planning for the future, are concerned.

Thus we are faced with an all-important and unavoidable question: If capitalism is an ecological and social dead end, what are the basic characteristics of a sustainable society and how can they be achieved? Considering a whole new type of economy and society is not as utopian as one might think. As we discuss a different economic system, consider whether it is any more utopian or unlikely than what has been proposed by others to deal with the problems of actually existing capitalism. Creating an entirely different system, no matter how difficult and visionary it may seem, is a more realistic alternative than a head-in-the-sand view that refuses to recognize the incompatibility between unlimited capital accumulation and limited resources, or that denies capitalism's connection to social and ecological exploitation. Wresting control of the "rules of the game" of capitalism from the most powerful economic and political forces and then attempting to institute strict controls without otherwise altering the system may help somewhat but still leaves economic decisions in private hands with profitmaking still the overarching goal—and represents at best a slower path to destruction. A utopian reformism, which says you can fundamentally change the system without touching its power relations, is the greatest illusion of all.

Remember that the people in power—the power elite, or more accurately the ruling class—control the key sectors of the economy and most of the media, as well as dominating the government. Can we expect radical change from such ruling elements? Is a different, more democratic, egalitarian, and planned economic system more utopian than vainly hoping that a "regulated" capitalist system, with its inherent anti-environmental tendencies intact, can solve our environmental crisis? If ecological and social issues are to be part of the decision-making process, why not institute a social and democratic process that includes these concerns when investment decisions are to be made? To ask such a question, however, is to raise the issue of a truly revolutionary form of change—the transition to a new system altogether.

This new system needs to have at its core the rational and democratic regulation of the economy in ways that (1) create substantive equality; (2) meet the basic material and non-material needs of the people, now and for future generations; (3) enshrine the social—instead of private—use of nature in ways that enhance and preserve the environment; and (4) create a social climate in which people are actively engaged with one another and with their communities.

When there are clear goals, the only way to increase the odds of actually achieving them is by planning. Does it make sense for someone to build a house without having a plan as to what the house is to be like and what is needed to accomplish the project? Or imagine saying that you want to drive from New York City to some small town in California, but you are going to use random highways and directions to get there instead of a map or GPS system. Similarly, once society decides that it is critical to fulfill the basic needs of people, then—after some general agreement is reached as to what these needs are—a system that plans production and distribution is required in order effectively to achieve those ends.

Economic planning has gotten a bad name because of the highly bureaucratic and anti-democratic Soviet command economy. However, there have been many cases of successful planning; while non-planning at the societal level under capitalism has gotten us to the point where we are destroying the environmental conditions of our own existence and crippling human potential. Some planning exists even under capitalism. Corporations regularly plan production and distribution—even if it is only for the short-term future and their own profits, and in the context of a system that is anarchic overall. Communities commonly use zoning regulations to help direct the type of development that will occur in particular parts of the town or village and what type of infrastructure is needed to support its plan.

In addition, the United States government had important and successful national planning efforts during both the First and

Second World Wars. (Companies went along with planning efforts that limited their freedom of action—often grudgingly after pressure was applied—only because of the clarity of the needs for the war effort.) It is inconceivable to think that such a massive and rapid shift to a war economy as that which occurred during the Second World War would have been possible without planning and stringent controls on both industry and individual consumption. And it is inconceivable that the United States interstate highway system could have been built without considerable planning.

In some countries today, notably Venezuela, the government has been able to implement planning in some areas to improve social and environmental conditions for the vast majority, Thus Venezuela's Bolivarian Revolution has promoted a radical shift to community self-governance, decentralizing decisionmaking over basic community infrastructure and social provisioning to tens of thousands of communal councils, through which the mass of the population are able to participate in the satisfaction of community needs. In Cuba planning has helped to ensure that there are more doctors per capita than any other nation on Earth and to sustain a highly developed education system: real victories in a poor country that show up in the health and education status of the population. As World Wildlife Fund's *Living Planet Report* indicated, Cuba is the only country in the world with a high level of human development and a per capita ecological footprint below the world's average.[16]

Water, electricity, and sewage were traditionally provided by public agencies (with some degree of planning) in most countries, in what was sometimes called "municipal socialism."[17] Only relatively recently has this given way to privatization and letting the market system increasingly determine whether people have water to drink and electricity for their homes.

Let's say that we have a goal as a society of meeting the basic material needs of the entire population within a country. How can such essentials as adequate housing, food, clean water, sanitation, and clothing be provided in the absence of planning to make it happen? Without investment decisions under social control—in other words, economic as well as political democracy—at the community, regional, and multiregional levels, there is no way to reach a future of substantive equality and sustainability, meeting the material and non-material needs of people while preserving the environment.

The transition to an ecological and democratic economy will be difficult and will not occur overnight. This is not a question of storming the Winter Palace. Rather, it will be a dynamic, multifaceted struggle for a new cultural compact and a new productive system. The struggle is ultimately against the *system of capital*. It must begin, however, by opposing the *logic of capital*, endeavoring in the here and now to create in the interstices of the system a new social metabolism rooted in egalitarianism, community, and a sustainable relation to the earth. The basis for the creation of sustainable human development must arise *from within* the system dominated by capital, *without being part of it*, just as the bourgeoisie itself arose in the "pores" of feudal society.[18] Eventually, these initiatives can become powerful enough to constitute the basis of a new revolutionary movement and society.

David Harvey has usefully referred to the movement for transformative social change as a "co-revolutionary" process. A radical political movement he claims can arise in any number of spheres: the labor process, in the relation to nature, in social relations, out of daily life, etc. "The trick," he writes, "is to keep the political movement moving from one sphere of activity to another in mutually reinforcing ways," to create a total systemic action that reinforces itself.[19] This is what philosopher István Mészáros, author of *Beyond Capital*, calls the process of forming a new system of "social-metabolic control," in which the different aspects of the system are organically related. Capitalism has this self-reinforcing character, and any new form of radical egalitarianism or socialism that seeks to supplant it can only do so by creating an alternative mutually-reinforcing system—this time in accord with the long-term needs of humanity and the earth.[20]

President Hugo Chávez in Venezuela refers to this as the *elementary triangle of socialism*: (1) social ownership; (2) social production organized by workers; and (3) the satisfaction of communal needs. We can give this a more ecological cast by referring to the *elementary triangle of ecology*: (1) social use, not ownership, of nature; (2) rational regulation by the associated producers of the metabolism between human beings and nature; and (3) the satisfaction of communal needs—of present and future generations.[21]

The reason that the opposition to the logic of capitalism, ultimately seeking to displace the system altogether, will grow ever more imposing is that there is no alternative, if the earth as we know it, and humanity itself, are to survive. People will increasingly "wake up" as Harvey says, "to the probability that endless capital accumulation is neither possible nor desirable."[22] Here, the aims of ecology (sustainability) and socialism (substantive equality) will necessarily meet. It will become increasingly clear that the distribution of land as well as food, health care, housing, and other necessities should be based directly on fulfilling human needs and not be reliant on mere "market forces" and the control exercised by capital.

This is, of course, easier said than done. But it means making economic decisions through democratic processes occurring at local, regional, and multiregional levels. What is needed is the active mobilization on their own behalf of millions of people. We must face compelling issues. How can we supply everyone in a nine-billion-person world with the basic human needs of food, water, shelter, clothing, health care, and educational and cultural opportunities? How much of the economic production should be consumed and how much invested? How should the investments be directed?

In the process, people must find the best ways to carry on these activities so as to promote positive interactions with nature.

New forms of democracy will be needed, with emphasis on our responsibilities to each other, to our community, and to communities around the world. Accomplishing this will require socially involved planning at every level. This can only be successful to the extent that it is *of* and *by*, and not just ostensibly *for*, the people.[23] What is needed above all is a system of substantive equality—what Simón Bolívar called "the law of laws"—as the condition of substantive democracy and ecological sustainability.[24]

An economic system that is democratic, reasonably egalitarian, and able to set limits on consumption will undoubtedly mean that people will live at a significantly lower level of resource use than occurs in what is sometimes referred to in the wealthy countries as "a middle-class lifestyle." But a simpler way of life, though "poorer" in gadgets and ultra-large luxury homes, can be richer socially and culturally, reestablishing connections between people and between people and nature—with people working shorter hours in order to provide life's essentials. A large number of jobs in the wealthy capitalist countries (for example most forms of commercial advertising) are wasteful and nonproductive, aimed only at perpetuating profits and the profit system, and can be eliminated—and this alone means that the workweek might be considerably shortened in a more rationally organized economy.

Such an egalitarian, sustainable society, while using far fewer resources per capita, need not be impoverished in a social, cultural, or even economic, sense. Indeed, economist Juliet Schor has written of the sense of "plenitude" that can prevail in a world where life's most basic needs are addressed, everyone has enough, products are constructed for durability, and the wealth of society is shared within communities.[25]

The slogan sometimes seen on bumper stickers, "Live Simply So that Others May Simply Live," has little meaning in a capitalist society. Living a simple life, such as Helen and Scott Nearing famously did—demonstrating that it is possible to live a rewarding and interesting life while living lightly on the earth—does not help the poor under present circumstances.[26] However, the slogan will have real importance in a society under social (rather than private) control—when trying to satisfy the basic needs for all people.

Perhaps the community councils of Venezuela, where local people in groups of up to four hundred families decide the priorities for social investment in their communities and receive the resources to implement them, are an example of planning for human needs at the local level. These councils are being linked together into a broader form of organization that is becoming involved in production and distribution to help meet the basic needs of the member communities. This is the way that such important needs as schools, clinics, roads, electricity, and running water can be met. Also food processing and distribution can take place in or near the local community. In a truly transformed society, such community councils (or communal organizations) would interact with other community councils nearby, as well as regional and multiregional entities. And the use of the surplus of society, after accounting for people's central needs, would be based in large part on their decisions.[27]

The creation of a new sustainable system, which constitutes the aim of today's environmental struggles, must have as its basis the satisfaction of the basic material and non-material needs of all the people, while protecting the global environment, as well as local and regional ecosystems. The environment is not something "external" to the human economy, as our present ideology tells us; it constitutes the essential life support systems for all living creatures. To heal the "metabolic rift" between the economy and the environment means new ways of living, manufacturing, growing food, transportation, and so forth, that recognize that we are deeply embedded in the environment.[28]

All people in a sustainable society need to live fairly close to where they work and where their children go to school, in ecologically designed housing built for energy efficiency as well as comfort, and in communities designed for public engagement, with sufficient places, such as parks and community centers, for coming together and recreation opportunities. Better mass transit within and between cities is needed to lessen the dependence on the use of cars and trucks. Rail is significantly more energy efficient than trucks in moving freight (413 miles per gallon of fuel per ton versus 155 miles for trucks) and causes fewer fatalities, while emitting lower amounts of greenhouse gases. One train can carry the freight of between 280 and 500 trucks. It is estimated that one rail line can carry the same amount of people as numerous highway lanes.[29]

Industrial production and homebuilding, as world-renowned architect William McDonough has argued, need to be based on ecological design principles of "cradle-to-cradle," in which products and buildings are designed for lower energy input, and which rely to as great a degree as possible on natural lighting and heating/cooling, ease of construction, easy reuse, and manufacturing processes that produce little or no waste.[30] The precautionary principle should be adhered to throughout society: if there is no proof that something (such as a chemical) is safe, then do not use it.

Agriculture must be based on ecological principles and carried out by family farmers, working on their own, or by people collectively organized in larger cooperatives. One of the key elements of such a system would be to raise animals on the same farms that grow their feed. Producing food using ecologically sound practices has been demonstrated to be as productive or more so than large-scale industrial production, uses less energy, and has less negative impact on local ecologies. In fact, the mosaic created by small farms interspersed with native vegetation is needed to preserve endangered species and provide habitat for beneficial insects.[31]

A better existence for slum dwellers, approximately one-sixth of humanity, must be found. A system that requires a "planet of slums," as Mike Davis has put it, has to be replaced by a system that has room for food, water, homes, and employment for all.[32] For many, this may mean returning to farming, with adequate land and housing and other support provided.

Smaller cities may be needed, with people living closer to where their food is produced and with industry more dispersed and operating at smaller scale.

Evo Morales, president of Bolivia, captured the essence of the situation in his comments about changing from capitalism to a system that promotes "living well" instead of "living better." As he said at the Copenhagen Climate Conference in December 2009:

> Living better is to exploit human beings. It's plundering natural resources. It's egoism and individualism. Therefore, in those promises of capitalism, there is no solidarity or complementarity. There's no reciprocity. So that's why we're trying to think about other ways of living lives and living well, not living better. Living better is always at someone else's expense. Living better is at the expense of destroying the environment.[33]

The earlier experiences of transition to non-capitalist, post-revolutionary systems, especially in Soviet-type societies, indicate that this will not be easy. What we need—along with the movements to bring this about—are new conceptions of what constitutes viable post-capitalist societies—aimed at maintaining a rational metabolism between humans and the environment, while promoting economic and social justice.

This type of socialist society, being advanced in the twenty-first century, is sharply distinguished from the early abortive attempts of transitioning to post-capitalist systems. Twentieth-century revolutions typically arose in relatively poor, underdeveloped countries that were quickly isolated and continually threatened from abroad. Post-revolutionary societies in this early stage of the revolt against capitalism usually ended up being heavily bureaucratic, with a minority in charge of the state effectively rul-

ing over the remainder of the society. Many of the same hierarchi-
cal relations of production (such as Taylorism or so-called scientific management) that characterize capitalism were reproduced.
Workers remained proletarianized, and production was
expanded for the sake of production itself. Real social improvements all too often existed side by side with extreme forms of
social repression. Such societies may have been post-capitalist, in
a certain sense, but they never managed to overcome the more
fundamental antagonism of capital and labor, with the state often
taking on the role of the collective capitalist.[34]

Revolutions in the early twenty-first century still continue to
emanate primarily from the poor countries of the periphery—
with enormous, seemingly insurmountable, obstacles facing such
revolutionary struggles, which must simultaneously deal with
issues of imperialism, underdevelopment, and ecological destruction. Nevertheless, conditions have in many ways changed, and
there are growing attempts—in such countries as Venezuela and
Bolivia, and post-1991 Cuba—to generate a new society of substantive equality, human freedom, and ecological sustainability.

Everywhere we must strive to create a viable "movement
toward socialism"—one aimed at the creation of a democratically
planned society in which bureaucracy is kept in check, and in
which power over production and politics truly resides with the
people and their communities.[35] Just as new challenges that confront us are changing in our time, so are the possibilities for
human emancipation and ecological justice. The traditional con-
ception of the proletariat or working class rooted in production,
specifically in factory labor, must give way to a broader concep-
tion of an environmental proletariat, concerned with the totality
of material conditions, from the human relation to nature through
production, to the broader community environment.[36] Such a
new agent of social change appears to be emerging out of the historical process itself, as worsening ecological conditions in much
of the world, and the cruelties of capitalism and imperialism, are

combining to create a new revolutionary subject, in which the environment looms as large as issues of work and development. This is the meaning of revolution in our times.

We need to recognize that we as human beings are a part of nature, not apart from nature. Capitalist society's exploitation of the environment has its roots in the exploitation of labor. The formation of a community with nature—a respect for the natural world—is essential in forging an egalitarian human community. "The restricted attitude of men to nature," Marx wrote, "determines their restricted relation to one another, and their restricted attitude to one another determines men's restricted relation to nature."[37] An ecological revolution means breaking with the vicious circle of the exploitation of both people and nature.

When Reverend Jeremiah Wright spoke at *Monthly Review*'s sixtieth anniversary gathering in September 2009, he kept coming back to the refrain: "What—about—the people?" If there is to be any hope of significantly improving the conditions of the vast number of the world's inhabitants—many of whom are living hopelessly under the most severe conditions—while also preserving the earth as a livable planet, we need a system that constantly asks: "What about the people?" and "What about the local, regional, and global ecosystems on which we all depend?"—instead of "How much money can I make?" This is necessary, not only for humans, but for all the other species that share the planet with us—all those whose fortunes are intimately tied to ours.

If Bolívar were alive today, his motto might well be: "Equality and sustainability are the *laws of laws*." Without one there is no hope of the other. The traditional aspirations of socialism and ecology are increasingly united—in opposition to capitalism and environmental collapse. In this lies our greatest hope.

Peoples' Agreement
Acuerdo Pueblos

WORLD PEOPLES' CONFERENCE ON CLIMATE CHANGE
AND THE RIGHTS OF MOTHER EARTH

APRIL 22, 2010, COCHABAMBA, BOLIVIA

Today, our Mother Earth is wounded and the future of humanity is in danger.[1]

If global warming increases by more than 2 degrees Celsius, a situation that the Copenhagen Accord could lead to, there is a 50 percent probability that the damage caused to our Mother Earth will be completely irreversible. Between 20 and 30 percent of species would be in danger of disappearing. Large expanses of forest would be affected, droughts and floods would affect different regions of the planet, deserts would spread, and the melting of the polar ice caps and the glaciers in the Andes and Himalayas would worsen. Many island states would disappear, and Africa would suffer an increase in temperature of more than 3 degrees

Celsius. Likewise, world production of food would diminish, causing catastrophic impact on the survival of inhabitants from vast regions in the planet, and the number of people suffering from hunger—a figure that already exceeds 1.02 billion people—would increase dramatically. The corporations and governments of the so-called developed countries, in complicity with a segment of the scientific community, have led us to discuss climate change as a problem limited to the rise in temperature without questioning the cause, which is the capitalist system.

We confront the terminal crisis of a civilizing model that is patriarchal and based on the submission and destruction of human beings and nature that has accelerated since the Industrial Revolution.

The capitalist system has imposed on us a logic of competition, progress, and limitless growth. This regime of production and consumption seeks profit without limits, separating human beings from nature and imposing a logic of domination upon nature, transforming everything into commodities: water, Earth, the human genome, ancestral cultures, biodiversity, justice, ethics, the rights of peoples, and life itself.

Under capitalism, Mother Earth is converted into a source of raw materials, and human beings into consumers and a means of production, into people seen as valuable only for what they own, and not for what they are.

Capitalism requires a powerful military industry for its processes of accumulation and imposition of control over territories and natural resources, suppressing the resistance of the peoples. It is an imperialist system of colonization of the planet.

Humanity confronts a great dilemma: to continue on the path of capitalism, depredation, and death, or to choose the path of harmony with nature and respect for life.

It is imperative that we forge a new system that restores harmony with nature and among human beings. And for there to be balance with nature, there must first be equity among human beings. We propose to the peoples of the world the recovery, revalorization, and strengthening of the knowledge, wisdom, and ancestral practices of Indigenous Peoples, which are affirmed in the thought and practices of "Living Well," recognizing Mother Earth as a living being with which we have an indivisible, interdependent, complementary, and spiritual relationship. To face climate change, we must recognize Mother Earth as the source of life and forge a new system based on these principles:

- Harmony and balance among all and with all things
- Complementarity, solidarity, and equality
- Collective well-being and the satisfaction of the basic needs of all in harmony with Mother Earth
- Respect for the Rights of Mother Earth and Human rights
- Recognition of human beings for what they are, not for what they own
- Elimination of all forms of colonialism, imperialism, and interventionism
- Peace among the peoples and with Mother Earth

The model we support is not a model of limitless and destructive development. All countries need to produce the goods and services necessary to satisfy the fundamental needs of their populations, but by no means can they continue to follow the path of development that has led the richest countries to have an ecological footprint five times bigger than what the planet is able to support. Currently, the regenerative capacity of the planet has been already exceeded by more than 30 percent. If this pace of overexploitation of our Mother Earth continues, we will need two planets by the year 2030.

In an interdependent system in which human beings are only one component, it is not possible to recognize rights only to the human part without provoking an imbalance in the system as a whole. To guarantee human rights and to restore harmony with nature, it is necessary to effectively recognize and apply the rights of Mother Earth. For this purpose, we propose a Universal Declaration on the Rights of Mother Earth, which includes:

- The right to life and the right to exist [*vida* = life]
- The right to be respected
- The right to regenerate Earth's bio-capacity and to continue its vital cycles and processes free of human alteration
- The right [of living things] to maintain their identity and integrity as differentiated beings, self-regulated and interrelated
- The right to water as the source of life
- The right to clean air
- The right to comprehensive health
- The right to be free of contamination and pollution, free of toxic and radioactive waste
- The right to be free of alterations or modifications of Earth's genetic structure that threaten its integrity or vital and healthy functioning
- The right to prompt and full reparation for human-caused violations of the rights acknowledged in this declaration.

Our shared vision seeks to stabilize the concentrations of greenhouse gases in order to uphold Article 2 of the United Nations Framework Convention on Climate Change, which calls for "the stabilization of greenhouse gases concentrations in the atmosphere to a level that prevents dangerous anthropogenic inferences for the climate system." Our vision, based on the principle of common but differentiated historical responsibilities, is to demand that developed countries commit to quantifiable goals of emission reduction that will allow return to concentrations of greenhouse gases of 300 ppm, and therefore limit the increase in average world temperature to a maximum of one degree Celsius.

Emphasizing the need for urgent action to achieve this vision, and with the support of peoples, movements, and countries, developed countries should commit to ambitious targets for reducing emissions that permit the achievement of short-term objectives, while maintaining our vision in favor of balance in Earth's climate system, in accordance with the ultimate objective of the convention.

The "shared vision" for "Long-term Cooperative Action" in climate change negotiations should not be reduced to defining the limit on temperature increases and the concentration of greenhouse gases in the atmosphere but must incorporate, in a balanced and integral manner, a combination of measures—financial, technological-adaptive, capacity building, and affecting production and consumption patterns, as well as other essential steps such as acknowledging the Rights of Mother Earth in order to re-establish harmony with nature.

Developed countries, as the main cause of climate change, in assuming their historical responsibility, must recognize and honor their climate debt in all of its dimensions as the basis for a just, effective, and scientific solution to climate change. In this context, we demand that developed countries

- Restore to developing countries the atmospheric space that is occupied by their greenhouse gas emissions. This implies the decolonization of the atmosphere through the reduction and absorption of their emissions.
- Assume the costs and technology transfer needs of developing countries arising from the loss of development opportunities due to living in a restricted atmospheric space.
- Assume responsibility for the hundreds of millions of people who will be forced to migrate due to climate change caused by these countries, and eliminate their restrictive immigration policies, offering migrants a decent life with full human rights guarantees in their countries.
- Assume adaptation costs related to the impacts of climate change on developing countries by providing the means to

prevent, minimize, and deal with damages arising from their excessive emissions.

• Honor these obligations as part of a broader debt to Mother Earth by adopting and implementing the United Nations Universal Declaration on the Rights of Mother Earth.

The focus must be not only on financial compensation but also on restorative justice, understood as the restitution of integrity to our Mother Earth and all its beings.

We deplore attempts by certain countries to annul the Kyoto Protocol, which is the sole specific legally binding instrument for the reduction of greenhouse gas emissions by developed countries.

We inform the world that, despite their obligation to reduce emissions, developed countries have increased their emissions by 11.2 percent in the period from 1990 to 2007.

During that same period, due to unbridled consumption, the United States of America has increased its greenhouse gas emissions by 16.8 percent, reaching an average of 20 to 23 tons of CO_2 per person. This represents 9 times more than that of the average inhabitant of the Third World, and 20 times more than that of the average inhabitant of Sub-Saharan Africa.

We categorically reject the illegitimate Copenhagen Accord that allows developed countries to offer insufficient reductions in greenhouse gases based on voluntary and individual commitments, violating the environmental integrity of Mother Earth and leading us toward an increase in global temperatures of around 4 degrees C.

The next Conference on Climate Change, to be held at the end of 2010 in Mexico, should approve an amendment to the Kyoto Protocol for the second commitment period from 2013 to 2017, under which developed countries must agree to significant domestic emissions reductions of at least 50 percent based on 1990 levels, excluding carbon markets or other offset mechanisms that mask the failure of actual reductions in greenhouse gas emissions.

We require first of all the establishment of a norm for all of the developed countries whereby each one of them can then be called upon to meet its individually assigned target, taking into account a comparison of their previous efforts, thus maintaining the Kyoto Protocol as the route to emissions reductions.

The United States, as the only Annex 1 country on Earth that did not ratify the Kyoto Protocol, has a significant responsibility toward all peoples of the world to ratify this document and commit itself to respecting and complying with emissions reduction targets on a scale appropriate to the total size of its economy.

We the people have the equal right to be protected from the adverse effects of climate change, and we reject the notion of adaptation to climate change and resignation to the impact of the historical emissions of developed countries, which must adapt their modes of life and consumption in the face of this planetary emergency. We see it as imperative to confront the adverse effects of climate change, and consider adaptation to be a process rather than an imposition, as well as a tool that can serve to help offset those effects, demonstrating that it is possible to achieve harmony with nature under a different model for living.

It is necessary to construct an Adaptation Fund exclusively for addressing climate change as part of a financial mechanism that is managed in a sovereign, transparent, and equitable manner for all states. This fund should assess the impacts and costs of climate change in developing countries and of the needs arising from these impacts, and to monitor support on the part of developed countries. It should also include a mechanism for compensation for current and future damages, loss of opportunities due to extreme and gradual climatic events, and additional costs that could occur if our planet surpasses ecological thresholds, such as those impacts that present obstacles to Living Well.

The Copenhagen Accord, imposed on developing countries by a few states, beyond simply offering insufficient resources, attempts as well to divide and create confrontation between peoples and to extort developing countries by placing conditions on access to adaptation and mitigation resources. We also assert as unacceptable the attempt in processes of international negotiation to classify developing countries for their vulnerability to climate change, generating disputes, inequalities, and segregation among them.

The immense challenge humanity faces in stopping global warming and cooling the planet can only be met through a profound shift toward the sustainable model of production used by indigenous and rural farming peoples, as well as to other ancestral models and practices that contribute to solving the problem of agriculture and food sovereignty. This is understood as the right of people to control their own seeds, lands, water, and food production, thereby guaranteeing, through forms of production in harmony with Mother Earth and appropriate to local cultural contexts, access to sufficient, varied, and nutritious foods, deepening the autonomous (participatory, communal, and shared) production of every nation and people.

Climate change is now producing profound impacts on agriculture and the ways of life of indigenous peoples and farmers throughout the world, and these impacts will worsen in the future.

Agribusiness, through its social, economic, and cultural model of global capitalist production and its logic of producing food for the market and not to fulfill the right to proper nutrition, is one of the principal causes of climate change. Its technological, commercial, and political approach only serves to deepen the climate change crisis and increase hunger in the world. For this reason, we reject free trade agreements and association agreements and all forms of the application of intellectual property rights to life, current technological packages (agrochemicals, genetic modification), and those that offer false solutions (biofuels, geo-engineering, nanotechnology, etc.) that only exacerbate the current crisis.

We similarly denounce the ways in which the capitalist model imposes mega-infrastructure projects and invades territories with extractive projects, water privatization, and militarized territories, expelling indigenous peoples from their lands, inhibiting food sovereignty, and deepening socio-environmental crisis.

We demand recognition of the right of all peoples, living beings, and Mother Earth to have access to water, and we support the proposal of the government of Bolivia to recognize water as a fundamental human right.

The definition of forests used in the negotiations of the United Nations Framework Convention on Climate Change, which includes plantations, is unacceptable. Monoculture plantations are not forests. Therefore, we require a definition for negotiation purposes that recognizes the native forests, jungles, and the diverse ecosystems of Earth.

The United Nations Declaration on the Rights of Indigenous Peoples must be fully recognized, implemented, and integrated in climate change negotiations. The best strategy and action to avoid deforestation and degradation and to protect native forests and jungles is to recognize and guarantee collective rights to lands and territories, especially considering that most of the forests are located within the territories of indigenous peoples and nations and other traditional communities.

We condemn market mechanisms such as REDD (Reducing Emissions from Deforestation and Forest Degradation) and its versions 1.0 and 2.0, which are violating the sovereignty of peoples and their right to prior free and informed consent as well as the sovereignty of national states, the customs of peoples, and the rights of nature.

Polluting countries have an obligation to carry out direct transfers of the economic and technological resources needed to pay for the restoration and maintenance of forests in favor of indigenous peoples' ancestral organic structures. Compensation must be direct and in addition to other sources of funding for developing countries; it must be outside of the carbon market, and must never serve as carbon offsets. We demand that countries stop initiatives in local forests based on market mechanisms and promising nonexistent and conditional results. We call on governments to create a global program to restore native forests and jungles, managed and administered by the peoples, using forest seeds, fruit trees, and native flora. Governments should eliminate forest concessions, should support keeping petroleum deposits in the ground, and should urgently stop the exploitation of hydrocarbons in forestlands.

We call upon states to recognize, respect, and guarantee the effective implementation of international human rights standards and the rights of indigenous peoples, including the United Nations Declaration on the Rights of Indigenous Peoples under ILO Convention 169, among other relevant instruments in the negotiations, policies, and measures used to meet the challenges posed by climate change. In particular, we call upon states to give legal recognition to our preexisting rights over our territories, lands, and natural resources, so as to make possible and strengthen our traditional ways of life and to contribute effectively to solving climate change.

We demand the full and effective implementation of the right to consultation, participation, and prior, free and informed consent of indigenous peoples in all negotiation processes, and in the design and implementation of measures related to climate change.

Environmental degradation and climate change are currently reaching critical levels, and one of the main consequences of this is domestic and international migration. According to projections, there were already about 25 million climate migrants by 1995. Current estimates are around 50 million, and projections suggest that between 200 million and 1 billion people will become displaced by situations resulting from climate change by the year 2050.

Developed countries should assume responsibility for climate migrants, welcoming them into their territories and recognizing their fundamental rights through the signing of international conventions that provide for the definition of "climate migrant" and require all states to abide by their determinations.

We call for the establishment of an International Tribunal of Conscience to denounce, make visible, document, judge, and punish violations of the rights of migrants, refugees, and displaced persons within countries of origin, transit, and destination, clearly identifying the responsibilities of states, companies, and other agents.

Current funding directed toward developing countries for climate change and the proposal of the Copenhagen Accord is infinitesimal. In addition to official development assistance and public sources, developed countries must commit to new annual funding of at least 6 percent of GDP to tackle climate change. This is viable, considering that a similar amount is spent on national defense and five times more has been put forth to rescue failing banks and speculators, which raises serious questions about global priorities and political will. This funding should be direct and free of conditions, and should not interfere with the national sovereignty or self-determination of the most affected communities and groups.

In view of the inefficiency of the current mechanism, a new funding mechanism should be established at the 2010 Climate Change Conference in Mexico, functioning under the authority of the Conference of the Parties (COP) under the United Nations Framework Convention on Climate Change and held accountable to it, with significant representation of developing countries, to ensure compliance with the funding commitments of Annex 1 countries.

It has been found that developed countries significantly increased their emissions in the period from 1990 to 2007, despite having stated that reduction would be substantially advanced with the help of market mechanisms.

The carbon market has become a lucrative business, commodifying our Mother Earth. It is therefore not an alternative for tackling climate change, as it loots and ravages the land, water, and even life itself.

The recent financial crisis has demonstrated that the market is incapable of regulating the financial system, which is fragile and uncertain due to speculation and the emergence of intermediary brokers. Therefore, it would be totally irresponsible to leave in its hands the care and protection of human existence and our Mother Earth.

We consider inadmissible that current negotiations propose the creation of new mechanisms that extend and promote the carbon market, for existing mechanisms have not resolved the problem of climate change nor led to real and direct actions to reduce greenhouse gases. It is necessary to demand fulfillment of the commitments assumed by developed countries under the United Nations Framework Convention on Climate Change regarding development and technology transfer, and to reject the "technology showcase" that only markets technology. It is essential to establish guidelines to create a multilateral and multidisciplinary mechanism for participatory control, management, and evaluation of the exchange of technologies. These technologies must be useful, clean, and socially sound. Likewise, it is fundamental to establish a fund for the financing and inventory of technologies that are appropriate and free of intellectual property rights. Patents, in particular, should move from the hands of private monopolies to the public domain in order to promote accessibility and low costs.

Knowledge is universal, and should on no account be the object of private ownership or exclusive private use, nor should its application in the form of technology. Developed countries have a responsibility to share their technology with developing countries, to build research centers in developing countries for the creation of technologies and innovations, and to defend and promote their development and application for living well. The world must recover and relearn ancestral principles and approaches from native peoples to stop the destruction of the planet, as well as promote ancestral practices, knowledge, and spirituality to recuperate the capacity for living well, in harmony with Mother Earth.

Considering the lack of political will on the part of developed countries effectively to comply with commitments and obligations assumed under the United Nations Framework Convention on Climate Change and the Kyoto Protocol, and given the lack of a legal international organism to guard against and sanction climate and environmental crimes that violate the rights of Mother Earth and humanity, we demand the creation of an International Climate and Environmental Justice Tribunal that has the legal capacity to prevent, judge, and penalize states, industries, and people that by commission or omission contaminate and provoke climate change.

We urge the peoples of the world to propose and promote deep reform within the United Nations, so that all member states comply with the decisions of the International Climate and Environmental Justice Tribunal.

The future of humanity is in danger, and we cannot allow a group of leaders from developed countries to decide for all countries, as they tried unsuccessfully to do at the Conference of the Parties in Copenhagen. This decision concerns us all. Thus it is essential to carry out a global referendum or popular consultation on climate change in which all are consulted regarding the following issues: the level of emission reductions on the part of developed countries and transnational corporations, financing to be offered by developed countries, the creation of an International Climate Justice Tribunal, the need for a Universal Declaration of the Rights of Mother Earth, and the need to change the current capitalist system. The process of a global referendum or popular consultation will depend on a process of preparation that ensures its successful implementation.

To coordinate our international action and implement the results of this "Peoples' Agreement," we call for the building of a Global Movement of Peoples for Mother Earth, which should be based on the principles of complementarity and respect for the diversity of origin and visions among its members, constituting a broad and democratic space for coordination and joint world-wide actions.

To this end, we adopt the global plan of action so that in Mexico the developed countries listed in Annex 1 respect the existing legal framework and reduce their greenhouse gas emissions by 50 percent, and that the different proposals contained in this agreement are adopted.

Finally, we agree to undertake a Second World Peoples' Conference on Climate Change and the Rights of Mother Earth in 2011 as part of this process of building the Global Movement of Peoples for Mother Earth and to react to the outcomes of the Climate Change Conference held at the end of 2010 in Cancún, Mexico.

Notes

Preface

1. Epicurus, *The Epicurus Reader* (Indianapolis: Hackett Publishing, 1994), 37.
2. Herman Daly, *Steady-State Economics* (Washington, D.C.: Island Press, 1991), 6, 149–51. Daly presented the Impossibility Theorem in terms of the impossibility of extending the U.S. mode of consumption to a planet with 4 billion people. Now there are 7 billion people and we are considerably overshooting the resources of the planet. Hence the impossibility of extending the U.S. mode of production and consumption to the population of the world as a whole as we approach a world with 9 billion-plus people is all the more obvious.
3. John Kenneth Galbraith, *The Economics of Innocent Fraud* (Boston: Houghton Mifflin, 2004).
4. Fred Magdoff and John Bellamy Foster, "What Every Environmentalist Needs to Know about Capitalism," *Monthly Review* 61/10 (March 2010): 1–30.
5. For more extensive treatments of the environmental problem, see John Bellamy Foster, Brett Clark, and Richard York, *The Ecological Rift* (New York: Monthly Review Press, 2010); Fred Magdoff and Brian Tokar, eds., *Agriculture and Food in Crisis* (New York: Monthly Review Press, 2010); Fred Magdoff, "Ecological Civilization," *Monthly Review* 62/8 (January 2011): 1–25.

1. The Planetary Ecological Crisis

1.   Frederick Engels, "The Part Played by Labour in the Transition from Ape to Man," in Karl Marx and Frederick Engels, *Collected Works* (New York: International Publishers) 25:460–61.

2.   Plato, *Timaeus and Critias* (London: Penguin, 1977), 133–34.

3.   Johan Rockström et al., "A Safe Operating Space for Humanity," *Nature* 461 (September 24, 2009): 472–75; and "Planetary Boundaries," *Ecology and Society* 14/2 (2009), http://ecologyandsociety.org. On the relation between planetary boundaries and the concept of ecological rift see John Bellamy Foster, Brett Clark, and Richard York, *The Ecological Rift* (New York: Monthly Review Press, 2010), 13–19.

4.   James Hansen, Reto Ruedy, Makiko Sato, and Ken Lo, "Global Temperature and Europe's Frigid Air," December 11, 2010, columbia.edu/~jeh1; "Global Surface Temperature Change," *Reviews of Geophysics* 48 (2010): 23; U.S. Department of Commerce National Climate Data Center, *State of the Climate Global Analysis Annual 2010,* accessed January 25, 2011, http://www.ncdc.noaa.gov/sotc/global/2010/13.

5.   James Hansen, *Storms of My Grandchildren* (New York: Bloomsbury, 2009), 164.

6.   Arctic Sea Ice News & Analysis, National Snow and Ice Data Center, September 15, 2010 report, http://nsidc.org/arcticseaicenews/.

7.   "Seas Could Rise Up to 1.6 meters by 2100: Study," *Reuters*, May 3, 2011.

8.   Hansen, *Storms of My Grandchildren*, 82–85; Richard S. J. Tol et al., "Adaptation to Five Meters of Sea Level Rise," *Journal of Risk Research* 5 (July 2006): 469.

9.   Agence France Presse (AFP),"Peru Glacier Collapses, Injures 50," April 12, 2010.

10.   World Glacier Monitoring Service/United Nations Environment Programme, *Global Glacier Change: Facts and Figures* (2008), http://grid.unep.ch/glaciers; Baiqing Xu et al., "Black Soot and the Survival of Tibetan Glaciers," *Proceedings of the National Academy of Sciences*, December 8, 2009, http://pnas.org; Carolyn Kormann, "Retreat of Andean Glaciers Foretells Water Woes," *Environment* 360, http://e360.yale.edu/; David Biello, "Climate Change Is Ridding the World's Tropical Mountain Ranges of Ice," *Scientific American Observations*, December 15, 2009, http://scientificamerican.com; Union of Concerned Scientists, "Contrarians Attack IPCC Over Glacial Findings, but Glaciers Are Still Melting," January 19, 2010, http://ucsusa.org.

11. Daniel Boyce, Marlon Lewis, and Boris Worm, "Global Phytoplankton Decline over the Past Century," *Nature* 466/7306 (July 29, 2010): 591–96; Gautam Naik, "Study Says Planet Warmed in 2000s," *Wall Street Journal*, July 29, 2010.

12. AFP, "UN Warns of 70 Percent Desertification by 2025," October 4, 2005; "Flooding Australia," *The Economist*, January 12, 2011, http://economist.com.

13. Omar Waraic, "Record Rains—But Pakistan Is Dying for Water," *The Independent* (UK), August 1, 2010.

14. Jesse A. Logan and James A. Powell, "Ghost Forests, Global Warming, and the Mountain Pine Beetle (Coleoptera: Scolytidae)," *American Entomologist* 47/3 (2001): 160–72; "80% of Whitebark Pines in Inner West Dead or Dying," *Climate Signals*, August 4, 2010, http://climatesignals.org/.

15. Shaobing Peng et al., "Rice Yields Decline with Higher Night Temperature from Global Warming," *Proceedings of the National Academy of Sciences* 101/ 27 (2005): 9971–75.

16. David B. Lobell, Marianne Bänziger, Cosmos Magorokosho, and Bindiganavile Vivek, "Nonlinear Heat Effects on African Maize as Evidenced by Historical Yield Trials," *Nature Climate Change*, published online March 13, 2011, www.nature.com/nclimate/journal/vaop/ncurrent/full/nclimate1043.html, accessed on March 25, 2011.

17. David B. Lobell, Wolfram Schlenker, and Justin Costa-Roberts, "Climate Trends and Global Crop Production since 1980," *Science*, published Online, May 5, 2011.

18. James Hansen, "Strategies to Address Global Warming" (July 13, 2009), www.columbia.edu/~jeh1/mailings/2009/20090713_Strategies.pdf; Hansen, *Storms of My Grandchildren*, 145–47.

19. Hansen, *Storms of My Grandchildren*, 83; Orrin H. Pilkey and Rob Young, *The Rising Sea* (Washingon: Island Press, 2009).

20. Rockström et al., "A Safe Operating Space for Humanity," 473; "Ocean Acification: 'Evil Twin' Threatens World's Oceans, Scientists Warn," *Science Daily*, April 1, 2010, http://science daily.com.

21. Rockström et al., "A Safe Operating Space for Humanity," 473 , and "Planetary Boundaries"; "Dobson Unit," http://theozonehole.com.

22. Richard Leakey and Roger Lewin, *The Sixth Extinction* (New York: Random House, 1995); Niles Eldredge, "The Sixth Extinction" (June 2001), http://actionbioscience.org/newfrontiers/eldredge2.html; Rockström et al., "A Safe Operating Space for Humanity," 473–74.

23. Frank Jordans, "17,000 Species Threatened by Extinction," *Associated Press*, November 3, 2009.

24. Monitra Pongsiri et al., "Biodiversity Loss Affects Global Disease Ecology," *Bioscience* 59/11 (2009): 945–54.

25. Rockström et al., "A Safe Operating Space for Humanity," 473–74; Foley, "Boundaries for a Healthy Planet."

26. Rockström et al., "Planetary Boundaries," 8, 15–16.

27. Maude Barlow, *Blue Covenant* (New York: New Press, 2007), 3.

28. Sudip Mazumdar, "Arid Land, Thirsty Crops," *Scientific American* vol. 304:26 (April 2011).

29. United Nations Food and Agricultural Organization, www.fao.org.

30. Rockström et al., "Planetary Boundaries," 8–9, 16–17.

31. Ibid., 9, 17–18.

32. Ibid., 9, 18–19.

33. Lindsey Hoshaw, "Afloat in the Ocean, Expanding Islands of Trash," *New York Times*, November 10, 2009.

34. Jennifer Ackerman, "Plastic Surf: The Unhealthful Afterlife of Toys and Packaging," *Scientific American* 303/2: 88–89 (August 2010).

35. U.S. Department of Agriculture, Agricultural Marketing Service, *Pesticide Data Program, Annual Summary, Calendar Year 2008* (December 2009). www.ams.usda.gov/AMSv1.0/getfile?dDocName =STELPRDC5081750.

36. Bobbi Chase Wilding, Kathy Curtis, Kirsten Welker-Hood, *Hazardous Chemicals in Health Care: A Snapshot of Chemicals in Doctors and Nurses,* Physicians for Social Responsibility, www.psr.org.

37. "Flame Wars; Chemical Pollution and Fertility," *The Economist*, January 30, 2010.

38. Philip J. Landrigan, "What Causes Autism? Exploring the Environmental Contribution," *Current Opinion in Pediatrics* 22/2 (2010): 219–225.

39. Maryse F. Bouchard, David C. Bellinger, Robert O. Wright, and Marc G. Weisskopf, "Attention-Deficit/Hyperactivity Disorder and Urinary Metabolites of Organophosphate Pesticides," *Pediatrics*, May 17, 2010, http://www.pediatrics.org.

40. Lyndsey Layton, "Use of Potentially Harmful Chemicals Kept Secret under Law," *Washington Post,* January 4, 2010.

41. Editors, "Chemical Control," *Scientific American*, April 2010, http://www.scientificamerican.com/article.cfm?id=chemical-controls.

42. David A. Fahrenthold, "Environmental Protection Agency Will List Bisphenol 'Chemical of Concern,'" *Washington Post,* March 30, 2010.

43. David Leonhardt, "Weak Rules on Toxins and Safety," *New York Times*, March 30, 2010.

44.   LaSalle D. Leffall Jr. and Margaret L. Kripke, *Reducing Environmental Cancer Risk: What We Can Do Now*, U.S. Department of Health and Human Services, National Institutes of Health, National Cancer Institute, April 2010.

45.   Rachel Carson, *Lost Woods* (Boston: Beacon Press, 1998), 210.

2. Business as Usual: The Road to Planetary Destruction

1.   Barry Commoner, *Making Peace with the Planet* (New York: New Press, 1992), ix.

2.   Donella H. Meadows, Dennis L. Meadows, Jorgen Randers, and William W. Behrens. *The Limits to Growth: A Report for the Club of Rome's Project on the Predicament of Mankind* (New York: New American Library, 1972), 29. See also Donella H. Meadows, Jorgen Randers, and Dennis L. Meadows, *The Limits to Growth: The Thirty-Year Update* (White River Junction, VT: Chelsea Green Publishing Company, 2004).

3.   Erik Assadourian, "The Rise and Fall of Consumer Cultures," in Worldwatch Institute, *State of the World, 2010* (New York: W. W. Norton, 2010), 6.

4.   Arthur B. Kennickell, "Ponds and Streams: Wealth and Income in the U.S., 1989 to 2007," Federal Reserve Board Working Paper, 2009-13 (2009), 55, 63; Matthew Miller and Duncan Greenberg, eds., "The Richest People in America" (2009), http://forbes.com.

5.   Epicurus, "The Vatican Collection," *The Epicurus Reader* (Indianapolis: Hackett, 1994), 39.

6.   Anup Shah, "Poverty Facts and Stats," *Global Issues*, last updated September 20, 2010, accessed January 14, 2011, http://www.globalissues.org.

7.   Gus Speth, "Toward a New Economy and a New Politics," *Solutions* 1/5 (2010): 33–41, http://www.thesolutionsjournal.com/node/619.

8.   Curtis White, "Barbaric Heart: Capitalism and the Crisis of Nature," *Orion* (May–June 2009), http://www.orionmagazine.org.

9.   "UN Forecasts 10.1 Billion People by Century's End," *New York Times*, March 3, 2011.

10.   Chico Harlan, "Strict Immigration Rules May Threaten Japan's Future," *Washington Post*, July 28, 2010.

11.   Herman E. Daly, *Steady-State Economics* (Washington, D.C.: Island Press, 1991), 149–51; Mathis Wackernagel, "Ecological Footprints," *Living on the Earth*, November 9, 2007, http://www.loe.org.

12.   Stephen Pacala, "Equitable Solutions to Greenhouse Warming: On the Distribution of Wealth, Emissions and Responsibility within and

between Nations," paper presented to International Institute for Applied Systems Analysis at Conference on Global Development: Science and Policies for the Future, Vienna, Austria, November 14–15, 2007.

13. Herman E. Daly, *Steady-State Economics* (Washington, D.C.: Island Press, 1991), 107; Commoner, *The Closing Circle.*

14. Donella Meadows, Jorgen Randers, and Dennis Meadows, *Limits to Growth: The Thirty-Year Update* (White River Junction, VT: Chelsea Green, 2004), 223–24.

15. U.S. Department of Labor, Bureau of Labor Statistics, "Consumer Expenditures in 2008," March 2010, Table 1; Michael Dawson, "Transportation Inequality in America," March 2, 2010, http://www.deathbycar.info; Hugh MacKenizie, Hugh Messinger, and Rick Smith, *Size Matters: Canada's Ecological Footprint*, Canada Centre for Policy Alternatives, June 2008, http://www.GrowingGap.ca.

16. G. Wiliam Domhoff, "Wealth, Income, and Power," January 2011, http://sociology.ucsc.edu/whorulesamerica/power/wealth.html; David Cay Jonson, "Income Gap Is Widening," *New York Times*, March 29, 2007.

3. The Growth Imperative of Capitalism

1. Paul M. Sweezy, "Capitalism and the Environment," *Monthly Review* volume 41, no. 2 (June 1989): 8.

2. Karl Marx, *Capital* (London: Vintage, 1976), 1: 742, and "Wage Labour and Capital," in *The Marx-Engels Reader* (New York: W. W. Norton, 1978), 213.

3. Richard Levins, "Why Programs Fail," *Monthly Review*: March 2010.

4. K. William Kapp, *The Social Costs of Private Enterprise* (New York: Shocken Books, 1971), 231.

5. James Gustave "Gus" Speth, "Towards a New Economy and a New Politics," *Solutions* 1/5 (2010): 33–41, http://www.thesolutionsjournal.com/node/619.

6. Donella H. Meadows, Dennis L. Meadows, Jørgen Randers, and William W. Behrens III, *The Limits to Growth* (New York: New American Library, 1972), 46.

7. On Marx's general formula of capital (M–C–M′), see Paul M. Sweezy, *Four Lectures on Marxism* (New York: Monthly Review Press, 1981), 28–31. For a discussion of Keynes's use of the same formula, see John Bellamy Foster, "The Financialization of Accumulation," *Monthly Review* 62/5 (October 2010): 3–6.

8.   John Schmitt and Nathan Lane, *An International Comparison of Small Business Employment* (Washington, D.C.: Center for Economic and Policy Research, 2009), 1.

9.   "Project Pack: Green Mountain Coffee Roasters," http://www.appreciativeinquiry.case.edu/practice/ppGreenMountain.cfm, accessed January 26, 2011.

10. Lauren Coleman-Lochner, "Green Mountain to Buy Van Houtte for C$915 Million," *Bloomberg Business Week*, September 14, 2010, http://www.businessweek.com/news/2010-09-14/green-mountain-to-buy-van-houtte-for-c-915-million.html; Associated Press, "Green Mountain to buy Van Houtte for $890 million," *ABC News*, September 14, 2010, http://abcnews.go.com/Business/wireStory?id=11631850.

11. WholeFoodsMarket.com, "Company History," http://www.wholefoodsmarket.com/company/history.php, accessed April 23, 2011.

12. Clorox Company, "Clorox to Acquire Burt's Bees; Expands into Fast-Growing Natural Personal Care," press release, October 31, 2007, http://investors.thecloroxcompany.com/releasedetail.cfm?ReleaseID=272197.

13. "M&A Deals Hit a Record $1.57 Trillion in 2007," *New York Times*, December 21, 2007.

14. Joseph A. Schumpter, *Capitalism, Socialism and Democracy* (New York: Harper and Brothers, 1942), 90.

15. U.S. Census Bureau, American FactFinder (2011), "Economic Census," 2007, and "Shipments Share of 4, 8, 20, & 50 Largest Companies in each SIC: 1992–1947," http://census.gov/econ/concentration.html. Beginning in 1997, the Standard Industrial Classification (SIC) system was replaced by the North American Industrial Classification System (NAICS), so these years are not strictly comparable in terms of the absolute number of industries. The Census Bureau is required by law to redact data when the concentration ratios are high enough to reveal the identity of a monopolist. In the calculations above, four industries with redacted four-firm concentration ratios (NAICS codes: 311919, 311930, 315221, 337129) were added to the total since the value must be close to one hundred percent.

16. See the data and analysis in John Bellamy Foster, Robert W. McChesney, and R. Jamil Jonna, "Monopoly and Concentration in 21st Century Capitalism," *Monthly Review* 62:11 (April 2011): 3–8.

17. "Big Food," *New York Times*, January 24, 2010.

18. Ellen Byron, "P&G Puts Up Its Dukes over Pricing," *Wall Street Journal*, April 29, 2010.

19. Frank V. Cespedes, Elliot B. Ross, and Benson P. Shapiro, "Raise Your Prices!," *Wall Street Journal*, May 24, 2010.

20. Andrew Simms, Victoria Johnson, Joe Smith, and Susanna Mitchell, *The Consumption Explosion: The Third UK Interdependence Report* (London: New Economics Foundation, 2009), http://www.neweconomics.org/sites/neweconomics.org/files/The_Consumption_Explosion_1.pdf.

21. John Kenneth Galbraith, *The Economics of Peace and Laughter* (New York: New American Library, 1971), 75-77.

22. Joseph A. Schumpeter, *Business Cycles,* vol. 1 (New York: McGraw Hill, 1939), 73.

23. Victor Lebow, "Price Competition in 1955," *Journal of Retailing* 31/1 (Spring 1955).

24. "Supermarket Facts, Industry Overview 2009," Food Marketing Institute, http://www.fmi.org/facts_figs/?fuseaction=superfact.

25. Ellen Byron, "Razor Burn: A Flood of Fancy Shavers Leaves Some Men Feeling Nicked," *Wall Street Journal,* July 12, 2010.

26. See the data in Robert W. McChesney, John Bellamy Foster, Hannah Holleman, and Inger Stole, "The Sales Effort and Monopoly Capital," *Monthly Review* 60/11 (April 2009): 6.

27. Amy Chozick, "What Your TV Is Telling You to Do," *Wall Street Journal*, April 7, 2010.

28. Mir Rooshanak, "Will You Sign Up for AT&T's New Location-Based Marketing Service?" U Printing.com, March 2, 2011, http://smallbusiness.uprinting.com.

29. Emily Steel and Julia Angwin, "On the Web's Cutting Edge, Anonymity in Name Only," *Wall Street Journal*, August 4, 2010.

30. Brooks Barnes, "Disney Looking into Cradle for Customers," *New York Times*, February 6, 2011.

31. Ibid.

32. Natasha Singer, "In a Graying Population, Business Opportunity," *New York Times*, February 5, 2011.

33. "U.S. Marketing Spending Exceeded $1 Trillion in 2005," Metrics Business and Market Intelligence, June 26, 2006, http://www.metrics2.com/blog/2006/06/26/us_marketing_spending_exceeded_1_trillion_in_2005.html. According to the above article, "Blackfriars collected data from 300 senior business excecutives about their marketing budget, attitudes, and spending. Blackfriars then correlated this data with overall business spending information collected by the 2001 U.S. Census and with gross domestic product data provided by the U.S. Bureau of Economic Analysis." See also Michael Dawson, *The Consumer Trap* (Chicago: University of Illinois, 2005), 1.

34. U.S. Department of Education, "Charts—10 Facts about K-12," Ed.gov, http://www2.ed.gov/about/overview/fed/10facts/edlite-chart.html.

35. Justin Lahart and Rachel Dodes, "Consumers Tighten Belts," *Wall Street Journal*, June 12, 2010.

36. For statistical sources and analysis see John Bellamy Foster, Robert W. McChesney, and R. Jamil Jonna, "Monopoly and Competition in Twenty-First Century Capitalism," *Monthly Review* 62: 11 (April 2011): 6–7.

37. For treatments of the role of speculation and debt in the U.S. economy, see John Bellamy Foster and Fred Magdoff, *The Great Financial Crisis* (New York: Monthly Review Press, 2009); and Fred Magdoff and Michael Yates, *The ABCs of the Economic Crisis* (New York: Monthly Review Press, 2009).

38. The inescapable contradictions of those who believe that a capitalist system can expand profits and prosper *without economic growth* and at the same time without in any way compromising the conditions of the majority of the population are evident in abundance in Philip Lawn's "Is Steady-State Capitalism Viable? A Review of the Issues and an Answer in the Affirmative," *The Annals of the New York Academy of Sciences* 1219 (2001): 1–25. Flying in the face of the entire history of economic thought (right, left, and center), and expunging both history and logic from his analysis, Lawn simply declares that profits can be created *ad infinitum* wihout either growth or reductions in the living standards of non-profit recipients. Profits, a *quantitative element*, can magically be generated in the economy as a whole, he tells us, through *qualitative improvements*, without net capital formation or growth.

39. Catherine Rampell, "With Recovery Slowing, the Jobs Outlook Dims," *New York Times*, July 30, 2010.

40. Neil Irwin and Sonja Ryst, "GDP Report: Economic Growth Slows with 2.4 Percent Rate in Second Quarter," *Washington Post*, July 31, 2010.

4. The Environment and Capitalism

1. Paul M. Sweezy, "Capitalism and the Environment," *Monthly Review* 41/2 (June 1989): 6.

2. Erik Eckholm, "Project's Fate May Predict the Future of Mining," *New York Times*, July 14, 2010.

3. See John Bellamy Foster, *Ecology Against Capitalism* (New York: Monthly Review Press, 2002), 131.

4. PricewaterhouseCoopers and The Grocery Manufacturers Association, *The Food, Beverage, and Consumer Products Industry: Achieving Superior Financial Performance in a Challenging*

Economy—2008, http://www.gmabrands.com/publica tions/GMA-PwC2008FinancialPerformanceReport.pdf.

5.   Vikas Bajaj, "In India, Wal-Mart Goes to the Farm," *New York Times,* April 12, 2010.

6.   Ylan Q. Mui, "As Growth in U.S. Slows, Wal-Mart Puts More Emphasis on Foreign Stores," *Washington Post,* June 8, 2010.

7.   Christina Passariello, "Carrefour Tries a Booster for Tiring Hypermarkets," *Wall Street Journal,* August 25, 2010.

8.   Mui, "As Growth in U.S. Slows, Wal-Mart Puts More Emphasis on Foreign Stores."

9.   *Economic Report of the President 2010,* data in Table B. 91: Corporate Profits by Industry, 1960–2009, *United States Government Printing House.*

10.   John Vidal, "Fears for the World's Poor Countries as the Rich Grab Land to Grow Food," *Guardian,* July 3, 2009; David Smith, "The Food Rush: Rising Demand in China and West Sparks African Land Grab," *Guardian,* July 3, 2009.

11.   Angus Maddison, *The World Economy: A Millennial Perspective* (Paris: Development Centre, OECD, 2001), 125–26; UNCSTADstat, "Nominal and Real GDP, Total and Per Capita, Annual, 1970–2009 (US Dollars at constant prices [2005] and constant exchange rates [2005])" and "Total population, Annual, 1950–2050," http://unctad-stat.unctad.org. UNCTAD only provides aggregate GDP per capita data for the G8, but the series is discontinuous because data for Russia are only available from 1992 to present. For the G7 figures, we excluded Russia and manually calculated GDP per capita using total GDP and population. Today the Least Developed Countries, as designated by the UN, include thirty-three in Africa, fourteen in Asia, and one in Latin America and the Caribbean.

12.   See Harry Magdoff, *Imperialism: From the Colonial Age to the Present* (New York: Monthly Review Press, 1978).

13.   For a brief discussion of European expansion, see Harry Magdoff and Fred Magdoff, "Approaching Socialism," *Monthly Review* 57/3 (July–August 2005): 19–61. On the relation of oil and gas to the wars in Iraq and Afghanistan, see Michael T. Klare, *Rising Powers, Shrinking Planet: The New Geopolitics of Energy* (New York: Metropolitan Books, 2008).

14.   See John Bellamy Foster, "A Warning for Africa: The New U.S. Imperial Grand Strategy," *Monthly Review* 58/2 (June 2006): 1–10.

15.   C. Wright Mills, *The Power Elite* (New York: Oxford University Press, 1956), 222; Andrew J. Bacevich, "The Tyranny of Defense Inc.," *Atlantic,* January/February 2011, http://www.theatlantic.com.

16. British Petroleum, *BP Statistical Review of World Energy*, June 2009, http://www.bp.com; John Bellamy Foster, *The Ecological Revolution* (New York: Monthly Review Press, 2009), 85–105.

17. David A. Vaccari, "Phosphorus: A Looming Crisis," *Scientific American*, June 2009, 54–59.

18. Karl Marx, *Capital*, vol. 1 (London: Penguin, 1976), 637.

19. Liam Pleven, "Pentagon in Race for Raw Materials," *Wall Street Journal*, May 3, 2010.

20. Paul Ziobro, "Restaurants Mobilize to Save Fisheries," *Wall Street Journal*, July 12, 2010.

21. Kai Olson-Sawyer, "Groundwater Use Increasing Sea Level Rise," in *SeaWeb's Ocean Update*, 15, no. 20, October 5, 2010. A description of Bierkens, M.F.P. et al., in press. "A Worldwide View of Groundwater Depletion," *Geophysical Research Letters*, http://www.seaweb.org/news/ou15_20.php#groundwater.

22. John Terborgh, "The World Is in Overshoot," *New York Review of Books* 56/19 (December 3, 2009): 45–57.

23. Wendell Berry, "What Else?," *The Solutions Journal*, July 15, 2010. http://www.thesolutionsjournal.com/node/669.

24. Frederick Engels, "The Part Played by Labour in the Transformation from Ape to Man," in Karl Marx and Frederick Engels, *Collected Works* (New York: International Publishers, 1975), vol. 25:463.

25. David Fahrenthold and Steven Mufson, "Documents Indicate Heavy Use of Dispersants in Gulf Oil Spill," *Washington Post*, August 1, 2010.

26. Campbell Robertson, "Gulf of Mexico Has Long Been Dumping Site," *New York Times*, July 29, 2010.

27. Richard Wray, "Abandoned Oil Wells Make Gulf of Mexico 'Environmental Minefield,'" *The Guardian* (UK), July 7, 2010.

28. Steven Mufson, "Federal Records Show Steady Stream of Oil Spills in Gulf Since 1964," *Washington Post*, July 24, 2010.

29. "Canada's Energy Industry: Tarred with the Same Brush," *The Economist*, August 5, 2010.

30. Bob Herbert, "An Unnatural Disaster," *New York Times*, May 28, 2010.

31. Ken Saro-Wiwa, *A Month and a Day* (New York: Penguin Books, 1995), 79.

32. U.S. Environmental Protection Agency, *Inventory of U.S. Greenhouse Gas Emissions and Sinks, 1990–2008*, EPA 430-R-10-006, April 15, 2010, ES-14.

33. Peter M. Vitousek, Paul R. Ehrlich, Anne H. Ehrlich, and Pamela A. Matson, "Human Appropriation of the Products of Photosynthesis," *BioScience* 36 (June 1986): 368–73.

34. Judith Warner, "The Way We Live Now: What the Great Recession Has Done to Family Life," *The New York Times Magazine*, August 6, 2010.

35. Adam Smith, *The Wealth of Nations* (New York: Modern Library, 1937), 14.

36. Duncan K. Foley, *Adam's Fallacy* (Cambridge, MA: Harvard University Press, 2006).

37. Noam Chomsky interview in Bill Moyers, *A World of Ideas* (New York: Doubleday, 1989), 58.

38. Benjamin R. Barber, *Consumed: How Markets Corrupt Children, Infantilize Adults, and Swallow Citizens Whole* (New York: W. W. Norton, 2007).

39. Albert Einstein, "Why Socialism?," *Monthly Review* 1/1 (May 1949), 14.

40. Bloomberg.com, "Profit 'Is Not Satanic,' Barclays Says, after Goldman Invokes Jesus," November 4, 2009.

41. Stephen L. Carter, "Profits We Should Cheer," *Washington Post*, July 30, 2009.

42. Thorstein Veblen, *The Instinct of Workmanship* (New York: Augustus M. Kelley, 1964), 25–26.

43. Frans de Waal, "Our Kinder, Gentler Ancestors," *Wall Street Journal*, October 3, 2009.

44. J. Kiley Hamlin, Karen Wynn, and Paul Bloom, "Social Evaluation by Preverbal Infants," *Nature* 450/7169 (November 22, 2007): 557–59; Nicholas Wade, "We May Be Born with an Urge to Help," *New York Times*, November 30, 2009. Some recent research in this regard is usefully summarized in Jeremy Rifkin, *The Empathic Civilization* (New York: Penguin, 2009), 128–34.

45. Einstein, "Why Socialism?," 10.

46. William Brandon, *The Last Americans: The Indians in American Culture* (New York: McGraw-Hill, 1974), 4, 6, 292.

47. Karl Polanyi, *The Great Transformation* (Boston: Beacon, 1944), 46.

48. John Dewey, "Human Nature," in *The Encyclopedia of the Social Sciences* (New York: Macmillan, 1937), vol. 7, 536.

49. See C. B. Macpherson, *The Political Theory of Possessive Individualism* (Oxford: Oxford University Press, 1962).

50. For a fuller discussion of these issues see Fred Magdoff and Harry Magdoff, "Approaching Socialism," 19–23.

51. Julia Werdigier, "British Bankers Defend Their Pay and Bonuses," *New York Times*, November 6, 2009.

52. For a contemporary view of the reserve army, see Fred Magdoff and Harry Magdoff, "Disposable Workers," *Monthly Review* 55/11 (April 2004): 18–35.

53. Matthew Miller and Duncan Greenberg, eds., "The Richest People In America" (2009), *Forbes*, http://www.forbes.com; Arthur B. Kennickell, "Ponds and Streams: Wealth and Income in the U.S., 1989 to 2007," Federal Reserve Board Working Paper 2009-13, 55, 63; Mike Hanlon, "How the World's Wealth Is Distributed—The Top Two Percent Own Half," November 6, 2006, www.gizmag.com; James B. Davies, ed., *Personal Wealth from a Global Perspective* (Oxford: Oxford University Press, 2008); Forbes.com, "World's Billionaires," March 8, 2007; Capgemini and Merrill Lynch Wealth Management, *World Wealth Report, 2009*, Introduction, http://us.capgemini.com; James Randerson, "World's Richest 1% own 40% of All Wealth, UN Report Discovers," *The Guardian*, December 6, 2006.

54. David S. Martin, "Toxic Towns: People of Mossville 'Are Like An Experiment,'" CNN, February 26, 2010.

55. U.S. Environmental Protection Agency, "EPA Releases Rulemaking Guidance on Environmental Justice," July 26, 2010. http://yosemite.epa.gov/opa/admpress.nsf/0/c00c43354d35367e85 25776c005ea8dc?OpenDocument.

56. Lisa P. Jackson, administrator, "Interim Guidance on Considering Environmental Justice during the Development of an Action," U.S. Environmental Protection Agency, July 26, 2010 http://www.epa.gov/ environmentaljustice/resources/policy/considering-ej-in-rulemaking-guide-07-2010.pdf.

57. Lawrence Summers, "Let Them Eat Pollution," *The Economist*, February 8, 1992. Full Summers quote analysis is to be found in John Bellamy Foster, *Ecology Against Capitalism* (New York: Monthly Review Press, 2002), 60–68.

58. Marlise Simons, "Oil Giant Fined for Shipping Sludge to Ivory Coast," *New York Times*, July 23, 2010.

59. Federal Reserve Board of San Francisco, "How Many Recessions Have Occurred in the U.S. Economy?" January 2008, http://www.frbsf.org; National Bureau of Economic Research, "Business Cycle Expansions and Contractions," January 17, 2010," http://www.nber.org.

60. John Cassidy, "Enter the Dragon," *The New Yorker*, December 13, 2010.

61. Barak Obama, "State of the Union Address to Congress," http://www.npr.org/2011/01/26/133224933/transcript-obamas-state-of-union-address, January 2011.

62. Ibid.

63. For a discussion of the power of finance in the U.S. political system, see Simon Johnson, "The Quiet Coup," *Atlantic Monthly*, May 2009.

64. Eric Lipton and Eric Lichtblau, "Fund-Raising before House Vote Draws Scrutiny," *New York Times*, July 14, 2010.
65. Dan Eggen and Kimberly Kindy, "Three of Every Four Oil and Gas Lobbyists Worked for Federal Government," *Washington Post*, July 22, 2010.
66. Jane Mayer, "Covert Operations: The Billionaire Brothers Who Are Waging a War Against Obama," *The New Yorker*, August 30, 2010.
67. See Robert W. McChesney, *The Political Economy of the Media* (New York: Monthly Review Press, 2008), 425–43.
68. Robert Reich, "Unjust Spoils," *The Nation*, July 19, 2010.
69. David Kocieniewski, "As Oil Industry Fights a Tax, It Reaps Subsidies," *New York Times*, July 3, 2010.
70. Johann Hari, "The Wrong Kind of Green" *The Nation*, March 22, 2010.

5. Can Capitalism Go Green?

1. Bill McKibben, *Earth* (New York: Henry Holt, 2010), 49.
2. Benjamin Barber, "A Revolution in Spirit," *The Nation*, February 9, 2009, http://www.thenation.com/doc/20090209/barber.
3. Paul Hawken, Amory Lovins, and L. Hunter Lovins, *Natural Capitalism* (Boston: Little, Brown, 1999). For a detailed critique of the ideology of "natural capitalism," see F. E. Trainer, "Natural Capitalism Cannot Overcome Resource Limits," *Minnesotans for Sustainability* (2001) http://www.mnforsustain.org.
4. Hawken, Lovins, and Lovins, *Natural Capitalism*; Al Gore, *Our Choice* (New York: Rodale, 2009), 346.
5. Worldwatch Institute, *State of the World 2010* (New York: W.W. Norton, 2010), 83–84; Herman E. Daly, "Economics in a Full World," *Scientific American* 293/3 (September 2005): 100–107.
6. James Gustave "Gus" Speth, "Towards a New Economy and a New Politics," *Solutions* 5 (May 28, 2010).
7. David Harvey, "Nice Day for a Revolution," *Independent* (UK), April 29, 2011.
8. On market inefficiencies and failures see Charles E. Lindblom, *The Market System* (New Haven: Yale University Press, 2001), 147–75. On the refusal of mainstream economics to confront the reality of market failure see John Cassidy, *How Markets Fail* (New York: Farrar, Straus and Giroux, 2009).
9. For a systematic discussion of how the market reduces the transparency of social relations see Bertell Ollman, "Market Mystification

in Capitalism and Market Socialist Societies," in Ollman, ed., *Market Socialism: The Debate among Socialists* (New York: Routledge, 1998), 81–121.

10. This critique is systematically developed in Karl Polanyi's classic *The Great Transformation* (Boston: Beacon Press, 1944).

11. James K. Galbraith, *The Predator State* (New York: Free Press, 2008), 19.

12. Joseph Schumpeter, *Capitalism, Socialism, and Democracy* (New York: Harper and Brothers, 1942); C. B. Macpherson, *The Life and Times of Liberal Democracy* (New York: Oxford University Press, 1977).

13. See especially Thomas Ferguson, *Golden Rule: The Investment Theory of Party Competition and the Logic of Money-Driven Political Systems* (Chicago: University of Chicago Press, 1995).

14. Rachel Carson, *Lost Woods* (Boston: Beacon Press, 1998), 210: and *Silent Spring* (Boston: Houghton Mifflin, 1994), 13.

15. Derrick Jensen and Aric McBay, *What We Leave Behind* (New York: Seven Stories, 2009), 201–6.

16. UN Secretary-General Ban Ki-moon, November 8, 2007, http://www.un.org/News/Press/docs/2007/sgsm11268.doc.htm.

17. Jensen and McBay, *What We Leave Behind*, 201–6.

18. Fredric Jameson, "The Future of the City," *New Left Review* 21 (May–June 2003): 76.

19. "Gucci Joins Other Fashion Players in Committing to Protect Rainforests," *The Independent*, November 5, 2009.

20. Daniel McGinn, "The Greenest Big Companies in America," *Newsweek*, September 21, 2009, www.newsweek.com.

21. Patric Wintour, "Green Consumerism Can Avert Climate Disaster, Say Top Firms," *The Guardian*, October 16, 2009.

22. Joel Bakan, *The Corporation* (New York: Free Press, 2004), 39–46.

23. Ibid., 109.

24. Tomás Mac Sheoin, "Chemical Catastrophe: From Bhopal to BP Texas City," *Monthly Review* 62/4 (September 2010): 21–33.

25. "Panel: BP and Others Made Risky Decisions before Spill," January 5, 2011, http:msnbc.msn.com.

26. Friedman quoted in Bakan, *The Corporation*, 41–42.

27. Martin Hickman, "Why Eco-Friendly Products Are Not as Green as They Appear," *The Independent* (UK), April 29, 2010.

28. Heather Rogers, *Green Gone Wrong* (New York: Scribner, 2010), 182.

29. Rachel Beck, "BP Gimmicks Fail to Hide Truth," Associated Press, July 11, 2010.

30. Beck, "BP Gimmicks Fail to Hide Truth."

31.   Eleanor Laise, "Oops: 'Socially Responsible' Funds Hold Big Stakes of BP," *Wall Street Journal*, July 17, 2010.

32.   The analysis in this paragraph draws on John Belllamy Foster, Brett Clark, and Richard York, *The Ecological Rift* (New York: Monthly Review Press, 2010), 388–90. See also Ray Anderson, Mona Amodeo, and Ida Kubiszewski, "Changing Business Cultures from Within," Worldwatch Institute, *State of the World, 2010*, 99–101; Michael Maniates, "Editing Out Unsustainable Behavior," in Worldwatch, *State of the World, 2010*, 125–26; Stacy Mitchell, "Keep Your Eyes on the Size: The Impossibility of a Green Wal-Mart," *Grist*, March 28, 2007, http://www.grist.org; Sarah Anderson, "Wal-Mart's New Greenwashing Report," November 20, 2007, http://www.alternet.org; Wes Jackson, quoted in Rogers, *Green Gone Wrong*, 191.

33.   Katherine Harmon, "How Does Geothermal Drilling Trigger Earthquakes?," *Scientific American*, June 29, 2009, http://www.scientificamerican.com/article.cfm?id=geothermal-drilling-earthquakes.

34.   Lisa Margonelli, "Clean Energy's Dirty Little Secret," *Atlantic Magazine*, May 2009.

35.   Fred Magdoff, "The Political Economy and Ecology of Biofuels," *Monthly Review* 60/3 (July–August 2008), 34–50.

36.   David A. Fahrenthold, "Chemicals that Eased One Woe Worsen Another," *Washington Post*, July 20, 2009.

37.   Foster, Clark, and York, *The Ecological Rift*, 169–82.

38.   Hannah Arendt, *The Human Condition* (Chicago: University of Chicago Press, 1958), 253.

39.   See Ulrich Beck, *Risk Society* (Newbury Park, CA: Sage Publications, 1992): and his *World Risk Society* (Malden, MA: Polity Press, 1999).

40.   For a powerful critique of risk management by a leading environmental scientist, see Mary O'Brien, *Making Better Environmental Decisions: An Alternative to Risk Assessment* (Cambridge, MA: MIT Press, 2000); also Charles Perrow, *Normal Accidents: Living with High-Risk Technologies* (New York: Basic Books, 1984).

41.   Perrow, *Normal Accidents*; James Lovelock, *The Revenge of Gaia* (New York: Perseus, 2006), 87–105; James Hansen, *Storms of My Grandchildren* (New York: Bloomsbury USA, 2009), 198–204. On the continuing dangers of nuclear power, even in its latest incarnations, see Robert D. Furber, James C. Warf, and Sheldon C. Plotkin, "The Future of Nuclear Power," *Monthly Review* 59/9 (February 2008): 38–48; and Mark Z. Jacobson and Mark A. Delucchi, "Providing All Global Energy with Wind, Water, and Solar Power, Part I," *Energy Policy* 39 (2011): 1154–1169, www.stanford.edu/group/efmh/jacobson/Articles/I/JDEn PolicyPt1.pd.

42. Klaus S. Lackner. "Washing Carbon out of the Air," *Scientific American* 302/6 (June 2010): 66–71.

43. American Physical Society, "Direct Air Capture of CO_2 with Chemicals," May 9, 2011, http://aps.org.

44. Hansen, *Storms of My Grandchildren*, 173–74, 193–94; and Hansen, "Coal-Fired Plants Are Death Factories," *The Observer*, February 15, 2009; Paul Epstein, et. al., "Full Cost Accounting for the Life Cycle of Coal," *Annals of the New York Academy of Sciences* 1219 (2011): 73–98; Kentuckians for the Commonwealth, "The Reality of the 'Clean Coal' Campaign," January 30, 2009, http://www.kftc.org.

45. John Broder, "From Theory to a Consensus on Emissions," *New York Times*, May 17, 2009. Emphasis added.

46. Friends of the Earth, "Subprime Carbon?," March 2009, http://www.foe.org/suprime carbon; and *A Dangerous Obsession*, November 2009, http://www.foe.co.uk; James Hansen, "Worshipping the Temple of Doom," May 5, 2009, http://www.columbia.edu/~jeh1/mailings/2009/20090505_Temple OfDoom.pdf; Larry Lohman, "Climate Crisis: Social Science Crisis," *The Corner House*, July 9, 2008, http://thecornerhouse.org.uk/resource/climate-crisis-social-science-crisis.

47. Rogers, *Green Gone Wrong*, 149–77; David Connett and Chris Stevenson, "Green schemes are 'wide open to major corruption'," *The Independent* (UK), May 1, 2011.

48. James Kanter, "Cap-and-Trade Is Beginning to Raise Some Concerns," *New York Times*, August 30, 2010.

49. Kanter, "Cap-and-Trade."

50. Hansen, "Worshipping the Temple of Doom."

51. See Paul Burkett, "Marx's Vision of Sustainable Human Development," *Monthly Review* 57:5 (October 2005): 34–62.

52. David Owen, "The Inventor's Dilemma," *The New Yorker*, May 17, 2010.

53. Owen, "The Inventor's Dilemma."

6. An Ecological Revolution Is Not Just Possible—It's Essential

1. Albert Einstein, "Why Socialism?" *Monthly Review* 1/1 (May 1949): 14.

2. Paul M. Sweezy, "Capitalism and the Environment," *Monthly Review* 41/2 (June 1989): 9.

3. Ibid., 9.

4. See James Hansen, *Storms of My Grandchildren* (New York: Bloomsbury, 2009), 172–77, 193–94, 208–22.

5.   See Aubrey Meyer, *Contraction and Convergence* (Devon: Schumacher Society, 2000); Tom Athansiou and Paul Baer, *Dead Heat* (New York: Seven Stories Press, 2002).

6.   Mark Z. Jacobson and Mark A. Delucchi, "Providing All Global Energy with Wind, Water, and Solar Power, Part I: Technologies, Energy Resources, Quantities, and Areas of Infrastructure, and Materials," *Energy Policy* 39 (2011): 1154–1169, http://www.stanford.edu/group/efmh/jacobson/Articles/I/JDEnPolicyPt1.pdf.

7.   On the world food crisis and its solution see Fred Magdoff and Brian Tokar, eds., *Agriculture and Food in Crisis* (New York: Monthly Review Press, 2010).

8.   See Maude Barlow, *Blue Covenant* (New York: New Press, 2007).

9.   Richard E. Leakey and Roger Lewin, *The Sixth Extinction* (New York: Anchor Books, 1995).

10. Franklin D. Roosevelt, 1944 State of the Union Address to Congress, http://www.presidency.ucsb.edu/ws/index.php?pid=16518.

11. Angela Park, *Environmental Justice and Climate Change* (Washington, D.C.: Environmental Support Center, December 2009), http://www.envsc.org/esc-publications/ESC%20everybody%20s%20movement.pdf.

12. Prensa Latina, "Chávez Stresses the Importance of Getting Rid of the Oil Rentier Model in Venezuela," *Mrzine*, January 11, 2010, http://www.mrzine.org.

13. Alec Loorz, "Why 16-Year-Old Alec Loorz is Suing the Government," *Good Magazine*, May 4, 2011.

14. Ryan Wishart and R. Jamil Jonna, "Power Shift: To Whom and from Whom," Part 3, April 14, 2011, http://itsgettinghotin here.org.

15. James Gustave Speth, *The Bridge at the Edge of the World* (New Haven: Yale University Press, 2008), 195.

16. World Wildlife Fund, *Living Planet Report* (2006), http://assets.panda.org.

17. Sidney Webb, *Socialism in England* (New York: Charles Scribner's Sons, 1901), 101–02; Lewis Mumford, *The City in History* (New York: Harcourt, Brace and World, 1961), 467–68.

18. Karl Marx and Frederick Engels, *Collected Works* (New York: International Publishers, 1975), 6:327; Karl Marx, *Capital* (London: Penguin, 1981), 3:447–48.

19. David Harvey, *The Enigma of Capital* (Oxford: Oxford University Press, 2010), 228–29.

20. István Mészáros, *Beyond Capital* (New York: Monthly Review Press, 1995), 45–46.

21.   See Michael Lebowitz, *The Socialist Alternative* (New York: Monthly Review Press, 2010); John Bellamy Foster, Brett Clark, and Richard York, *The Ecological Rift* (New York: Monthly Review Press, 201), 417.

22.   Harvey, *The Enigma of Capital*, 229.

23.   On planning, see Harry Magdoff and Fred Magdoff, *Monthly Review* "Approaching Socialism," 57, no. 3 (July-August 2005): 36–61.

24.   Simón Bolívar, *Selected Works*, vol. 2 (New York: Colonial Press, 1951), 603.

25.   Juliet Schor, *Plenitude: The New Economics of True Wealth* (New York: Penguin, 2010).

26.   See Helen and Scott Nearing, *Living the Good Life* (New York: Schocken, 1970). Scott Nearing was for many years the author of the "World Events" column in *Monthly Review*.

27.   See Iain Bruce, *The Real Venezuela* (London: Pluto Press, 2008), 139–75.

28.   On the metabolic rift see John Bellamy Foster, *The Ecological Revolution* (New York: Monthly Review Press, 2009), 161–200.

29.   C. James Kruse, Annie Protopapas, Leslie E. Olson, and David H. Bierling, "A Modal Comparison of Domestic Freight Transportation Effects on the General Public," Center for Ports and Waterways, Texas Transportation Institute, 2007, http://www.americanwater-ways.com; Mechanical Database website, Rail vs. Truck Industry, January 17, 2010, http://www.mechdb.com.

30.   William McDonough and Michael Braungart, *Cradle to Cradle* (New York: North Point Press, 2002). For a critique of McDonough for allowing his important contribution to be subverted by corporate priorities see Derrick Jensen and Aric McBay, *What We Leave Behind* (New York: Seven Stories Press, 2009), 61–73.

31.   See Miguel A. Altieri, "Agroecology, Small Farms, and Food Sovereignty," *Monthly Review* 61/ 3 (July–August 2009): 102–13.

32.   Mike Davis, *Planet of Slums* (London; Verso, 2006).

33.   Evo Morales interview with Amy Goodman, *Democracy Now*, December 17, 2009, www. democracynow.org/2009/12/17/bolivian_president_evo_morales_on_climate.

34.   See Paul M. Sweezy, *Post-Revolutionary Society* (New York: Monthly Review Press, 1980).

35.   "Movement Towards Socialism" is the name of the Bolivian socialist party led by Bolivian president Evo Morales. It is bringing together the indigenous critique of today's dominant order and ecological values, while drawing on many of the insights of classical Marxism.

36.   The fact that such a view was always implicit in clasical socialist theory can be seen by looking at Frederick Engels, *The Condition of the*

Working Class in England (Chicago: Academy Chicago Publishers, 1984). Engels's work focuses on the environmental conditions of the proletariat even more than on its factory conditions, in a manner that was common to the nineteenth-century working-class and socialist movement.

37.   Karl Marx and Frederick Engels, *Collected Works* (New York: International Publishers, 1975), vol. 6, 44.

Appendix: Peoples' Agreement (Acuerdo Pueblos)

1.   This document is taken from the English translation of the *Peoples' Agreement*, to be found on the Web page of the World Peoples' Conference on Climate Change. The translation has been altered slightly, with the help of Victor Wallis, to conform more fully to the Spanish original.

Index